HEAVY METAL
THUNDER

HEAVY METAL THUNDER

KICK-ASS COVER ART FROM KICK-ASS ALBUMS

JAMES SHERRY & NEIL ALDIS

CHRONICLE BOOKS
SAN FRANCISCO

This book is dedicated to Milo, Maisy, and Sadie, metal nuggets in the making, and to Vanessa and Jane, for putting up with years of metal hell. Hail Satan!

First published in the United States in 2006 by Chronicle Books LLC.

First published in Great Britain in 2006 by Mitchell Beazley.

Library of Congress Cataloging-in-Publication Data available.

ISBN-10: 0-8118-5353-5
ISBN-13: 978-0-8118-5353-8

Manufactured in Hong Kong

Cover design by Jacob T. Gardner
Cover photo © Jim Zuckerman/CORBIS

Distributed in Canada by Raincoast Books
9050 Shaughnessy Street
Vancouver, British Columbia V6P 6E5

10 9 8 7 6 5 4 3 2 1

Chronicle Books LLC
85 Second Street
San Francisco, California 94105

www.chroniclebooks.com

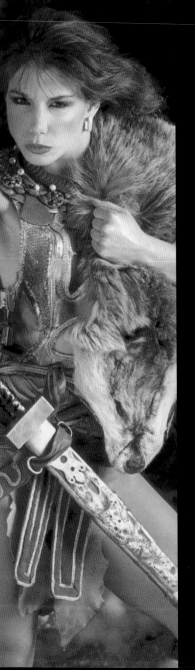

CONTENTS

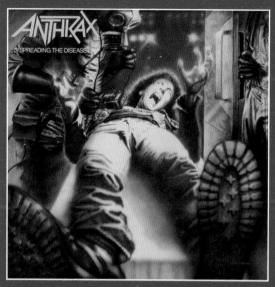

SPREADING THE DISEASE 1985

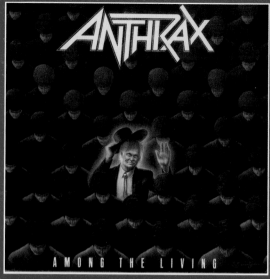

AMONG THE LIVING 1987

STATE OF EUPHORIA 1988

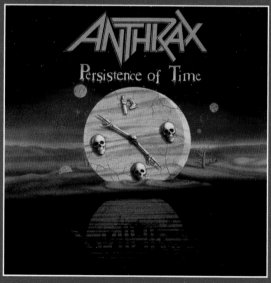

PERSISTENCE OF TIME 1990

FOREWORD

Album covers. Remember them? Those 12 x 12 pieces of cardboard that held a vinyl record? Vinyl? Don't even get me started on that.

Ah, the good old days, when you'd buy an album without ever having heard of the band. With the end of the vinyl era, the advent of the CD, and the death of the CD long-box, the perception of cover art has changed. In fact, the whole music business has changed drastically since the CD was born, but that's another story for another book.

Packaging used to rule all. A record had to have great art to even compete on the racks. You have to realize that people used to buy records solely based on artwork. I know it's hard to imagine that, especially in this pre-packaged, corporate, MTV spoon-fed world we live in, but that's the truth. I know first hand, my friends, because most of my favourite albums were purchased that way.

Let me take you back to 1975 as I walk into a record store with my father and feast my eyes on the cover of *Kiss Alive* for the first time. I was dumbstruck. It was Marvel Comics with guitars. They were larger than life real superheroes, and I got all that just from looking at the cover. It was everything an 11 year old who just started playing guitar could want a band to look like. They could have ended up sounding like shit, but it didn't matter. I had to have that record. I had to buy a birthday present for my father and all I had was ten dollars I had saved from my weekly allowance money. It was either buy the Kiss record or get my dad a gift, so I bought *Kiss Alive* and gave it to him for his birthday. He was very gracious accepting it and then handed it back to me and told me to go put it on. I was a member of the Kiss Army from that moment on and they became the reason I am sitting

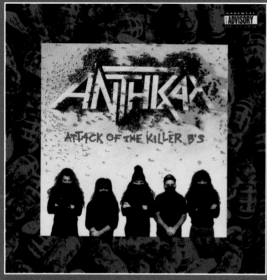

ATTACK OF THE KILLER B'S 1991   RETURN OF THE KILLER A'S 1995

here backstage now at the Anthrax/Judas Priest show typing this. The cover art to that record profoundly changed my life.

And speaking of Judas Priest, it was the cover art to their *Hell Bent For Leather* album that made me buy it and forever be in debt to the twin guitars of Tipton and Downing, which directly influenced what kind of band Anthrax would become.

Perhaps the best example of a band whose cover art directly connects with the fans is Iron Maiden. Their zombie icon "Eddie" was eye candy to any metal-head from day one. I bought the first Maiden record without ever having heard a note because of the living dead guy on the cover. Derek Riggs' creation became the must have T-shirt for every fashionable metal-head the world round. And the band is pretty damn great as well.

THE THREAT IS REAL 1998

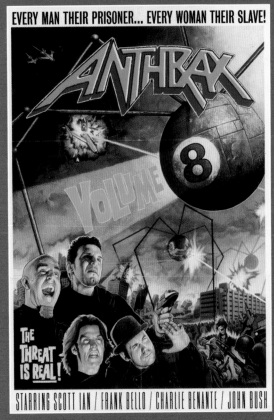

Inside gatefold

❝ Let me take you back to 1975 as I walk
into a record store with my father and
feast my eyes on the cover of *Kiss Alive*
for the first time. ❞

Sometimes cover art could trick you. I bought Motörhead's *Ace Of Spades* record because I thought the picture of them on the front cover looked cool. They looked like Mexican bandits. When I got the record home I was blown away by the ferocity and power of the band and I wondered who these Mexicans were and how could they play so fast? Lemmy ended up using that story in the liner notes of their live record.

I still browse the shelves of record stores looking for something to catch my eye, because I believe that a band that takes the time and effort to produce great art for their covers is a band that cares about their music and their audience. The cover is the first thing you see, and remember the old cliché: you can only make a first impression once.

Cheers,
Scott Ian

RETURN OF THE KILLER A'S 1999

WE'VE COME FOR YOU ALL 2003

1

FOR THOSE ABOUT TO ROCK....

The distant sound of thunder as the rain begins to fall. It gets louder, more foreboding, as the storm draws closer and lightning cracks overhead. Somewhere, a bell tolls, slow and regular. Something dark and sinister is heading this way.

Then it happens. The creation of heavy metal in a nutshell. A singular moment of crushing heaviness that will define the genre for years to come and rarely be bettered. As the thunder subsides, four dope-ravaged teenagers from Birmingham, England, known collectively as Black Sabbath, pound into the title track of their first self-titled album, grinding into a riff that is still the most menacing and frightening noise ever to have emerged from a fretboard. Ever. It's not subtle, it's not complex, it's just heaviness in its purest form, and it woke up the world to how truly dark and demonic music could sound.

It was 1969, the 60s were all but over. Charles Manson and his knife and fork-wielding buddies had put an end to peace and love. The Beatles were busy suing each other, the Rolling Stones were using gun-toting Hell's Angels for security. The optimism and hope of that decade had vanished, and as the 70s came down on everyone like a dark cloud, Tony Iommi, Ozzy Osbourne, Bill Ward, and Geezer Butler welcomed these uncertain times with open arms and riffs of thunder.

> What is this that stands before me,
> Figure in black that points at me,
> Turn around quick and start to run,
> Find out I'm the chosen one.
> "Black Sabbath" – Black Sabbath

BLACK SABBATH **BLACK SABBATH** 1970

Clearly Black Sabbath wasn't the first band to play loud guitars. The roots of metal can be traced through a host of classic rock bands. the Stooges, the Kinks, the MC5, the Who, Blue Cheer, Atomic Rooster, Black Widow, "Helter Skelter" by the Beatles; they all boasted heavy guitars and played their part in creating what would become Black Sabbath and, in turn, heavy metal. Sabbath's occult imagery, satanic lyrical overtones, and obsession with the darker side of life would become mainstays of heavy metal, the heart of the beast.

Ironically, Black Sabbath were dogged with as many lame album covers as they were classics. While the cover of their debut album featured the haunting image of a witch-like figure at the edge of a forest, which perfectly complemented the demonic sounds within, its follow-up, *Paranoid*, presented the decidedly unterrifying and remarkably silly cover of a man dressed in shorts and bright orange jerkin, sporting a helmet and waving a sword, like some angry cyclist on the rampage. The artist, Marcus Keef, who provided the artwork for the band's first three albums, chose to use a blurring effect, making the cover look as though you'd had one too many Jack and Cokes.

Perhaps the greatest Black Sabbath album cover of all is 1973's *Sabbath Bloody Sabbath*. Entitled "The Rape of Christ", this original artwork was painted by Drew Struzen, who would go on to create the most recognizable image of the 70s and 80s, the movie poster for the original *Star Wars* film. "The front of the cover represents a man dying on his deathbed," explained Ozzy back in January 1974. "There are all these distorted figures bending over him and gloating as he lies there. These figures are actually him at different stages of his life. He's a man of greed, a man who's wanted everything all his life and done all this evil stuff. But flip the album over, and the back represents the good side of life. The person dying on the bed has been really good to people. He's got all these beautiful people crying over him as he's dying. At the bottom of the bed, he has two tame lions guarding him. All in all, this represents the good and bad of everything."

BLACK SABBATH **PARANOID** 1970

BLACK SABBATH **VOLUME FOUR** 1972

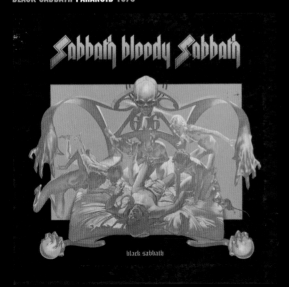

BLACK SABBATH **SABBATH BLOODY SABBATH** 1973

SABBATH BLOODY SABBATH Back cover

Drew Struzen's artwork here is both beautifully chilling and very heavy metal. Bands such as Deep Purple or Led Zeppelin – despite Jimmy Page's infamous obsession with the occult – and legendary satanist, Aleister Crowley, would not have been able to create album-cover artwork to rival *Sabbath Bloody Sabbath*. While many fans consider artists like Deep Purple and Led Zeppelin, together with acts like Uriah Heep, UFO, Thin Lizzy, and Rainbow as heavy metal bands, the fact is that Black Sabbath took the concept of heavy rock, as it was then known, and gave it a lethal dose of mercury, killing off heavy rock and spawning a new superhero for a new age – heavy metal – in the process.

However, in terms of heavy metal album covers, there are two hard rock bands who cannot be ignored: Australia's AC/DC and American legends, Kiss. Kiss, in particular, are the perfect example of the metal image taken to such an extreme that it actually became more important than the music. Without their make-up, monstrous stage shows and Gene Simmon's fire-breathing, blood-spitting theatrics, they would probably have sunk without trace after their first three albums. Take a look at the artwork for their 1976 classic *Destroyer*. It has everything you could want from a 70s proto-metal band. The band explode from a fiery pit of hell as they celebrate their triumphant victory, returning from their battles as saviours of rock. Very heavy metal. And then there's AC/DC's *If You Want Blood*. Yes, that's guitarist Angus Young, with his world-famous Gibson SG rammed into his stomach. Death by electric guitar. It doesn't get much more heavy metal than that.

From these beginnings, 80s metal went from the sublime to the ridiculous. You have German mini-metallers Accept's *Balls To The Wall*, possibly the most homoerotic cover art in the history of heavy metal – a genre not known for its tolerance of homosexuality. Then there's Handsome Beasts' fatty frontman Gary Dalloway sitting in a pigpen for the cover of their debut album, *Beastiality*. It's clear to see that though the metal of this period, known today as classic metal, may well have been over-the-top, cheap and trashy, it was always entertaining, as both bands and artists pushed back the barriers of taste.

KISS DESTROYER 1976

AC/DC **IF YOU WANT BLOOD** 1978

SAXON **SAXON** 1979

CEPT **ACCEPT** 1979

SCORPIONS **LOVEDRIVE** 1979

SAXON **WHEELS OF STEEL** 1980

WITCHFYNDE **GIVE 'EM HELL** 1980

ANGEL WITCH **ANGEL WITCH** 1980

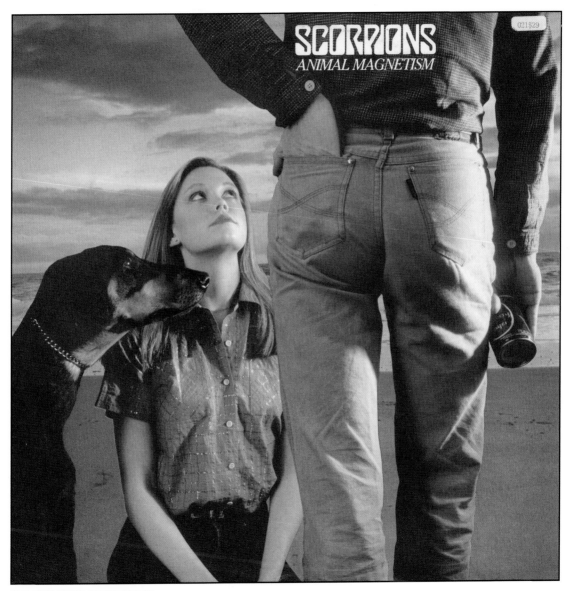

SCORPIONS **ANIMAL MAGNETISM** 1980

TYGERS OF PAN TANG **WILD CAT** 1980

SAMSON **HEAD ON** 1980

CIRITH UNGOL **FROST AND FIRE** 1981

BLACK SABBATH **MOB RULES** 1981

GIRLSCHOOL **HIT AND RUN** 1981

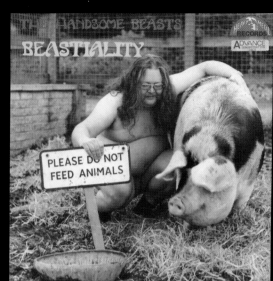

THE HANDSOME BEASTS **BEASTIALITY** 1981

JUDAS PRIEST **SCREAMING FOR VENGEANCE** 1982

FIST **BACK WITH A VENGEANCE** 1982

THE RODS **WILD DOGS** 1982

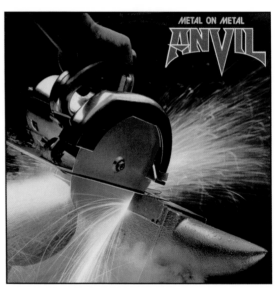

ANVIL **METAL ON METAL** 1982

DIAMOND HEAD **BORROWED TIME** 1982

OZZY OSBOURNE BARK AT THE MOON 1983

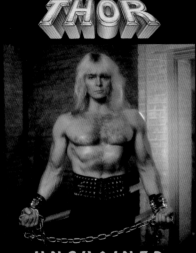

THOR UNCHAINED 1983

ACCEPT BALLS TO THE WALL 1983

ROCK GODDESS **HELL HATH NO FURY** 1983

DIO **HOLY DIVER** 1983

MSG **BUILT TO DESTROY** 1983

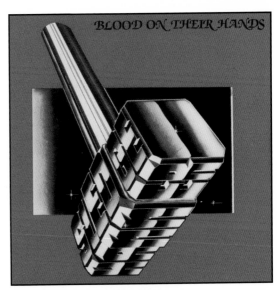

SLEDGEHAMMER **BLOOD ON THEIR HANDS** 1983

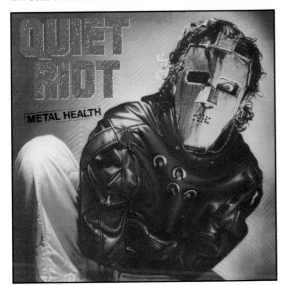

QUIET RIOT **METAL HEALTH** 1983

GRIM REAPER **SEE YOU IN HELL** 1984

MOTÖRHEAD

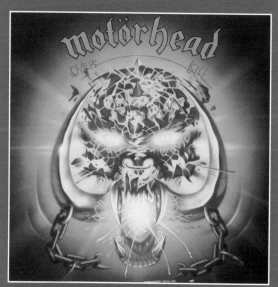

OVERKILL 1979

BOMBER 1979

To this day, Motörhead are still the loudest, dirtiest, most obnoxious rock band ever to have stalked the earth. Joe Petagno's Snaggletooth skull has adorned the majority of Motörhead's covers and, alongside Iron Maiden's Eddie The 'Ead, is one of metal's most recognizable images. British chain store Top Shop even sold Motörhead T-shirts featuring Snaggletooth as ironic rock wear for the fashionable.

Designer Petagno met Motörhead main man Lemmy while working for Hawkwind, a psychedelic heavy rock band from which Lemmy had

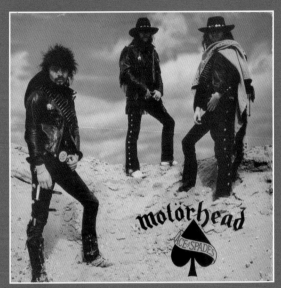

ACE OF SPADES 1980

ANOTHER PERFECT DAY 1983

been fired. Originally a song title Lemmy had penned and recorded with Hawkwind, he took the name Motörhead for his own band, asking Petagno to design its logo. Snaggletooth was born. Joe designed all of Motörhead's classic album covers, many of which featured this metal icon. However, Motörhead's most famous album, *Ace Of Spades*, sees the line-up of Lemmy, Fast Eddie Clarke, and Filthy Phil Taylor on the cover as roguish bandits, exuding an air of pure menace. It captures the no-compromise, in-your-face attitude of the band that has been the mainstay of its 30-year metal dominance.

MERCYFUL FATE
don't break
the oath

LEE AARON **METAL QUEEN** 1984   WENDY O WILLIAMS **WOW** 1984

ORAL **SEX** 1984

ARMORED SAINT **MARCH OF THE SAINT** 1984

EXCITER **LONG LIVE THE LOUD** 1985

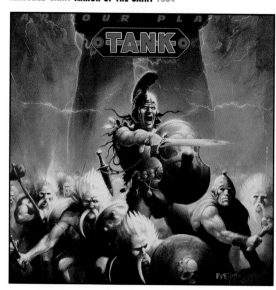

TANK **ARMOUR PLATED** 1985

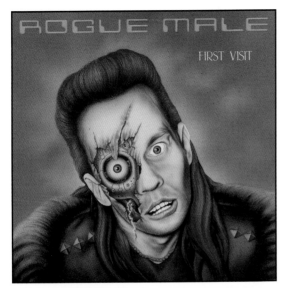

ROGUE MALE **FIRST VISIT** 1985

SEDUCER **'EADS DOWN SEE YOU AT THE END** 1986

TYRANT **RUNNING HOT** 1986

BATTLEAXE **POWER FROM THE UNIVERSE** 1986

RAVEN **THE PACK IS BACK** 1986

YNGWIE J. MALMSTEEN **TRILOGY** 1986

FASTWAY **TRICK OR TREAT** 1986

ALICE COOPER **RAISE YOUR FIST AND YELL** 1987

WARLOCK TRIUMPH AND AGONY 1987

JOE SATRIANI SURFING WITH THE ALIEN 1987

DANZIG **DANZIG** 1988

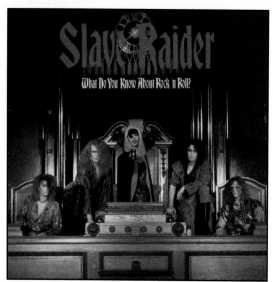

SLAVE RAIDER **WHAT DO YOU KNOW ABOUT ROCK 'N ROLL?** 1988

" King Diamond played every show in his trademark facepaint and, through his early work as lead vocalist with Mercyful Fate, became an influence on black metal. **"**

KING DIAMOND **CONSPIRACY** 1989

COMEDY BANDS

BAD NEWS **BAD NEWS** 1984

GWAR **SCUMDOGS OF THE UNIVERSE** 1990

You can call metal many things: stupid, ugly, noisy, violent, and base, and you'd be right. But unlike other genres, metal can laugh at its own absurdities. The most successful attempts at lampooning metal came with two movies, *This Is Spinal Tap* (1984) and *Bad News Tour* (1984). The soundtrack album to the former, *Smell The Glove*, simply had a plain black sleeve. "It's like: 'How much more black could this be?' And the answer is, 'None, none more black,'" said Nigel Tufnel, Spinal Tap's guitarist. When the band reformed in 1992 for *Break Like The Wind*, the cover perfectly represented the outlandish nature of metal bands.

HAUNTED GARAGE **POSSESSION PARK** 1991

SPINAL TAP **BREAK LIKE THE WIND** 1992

The English metal band Bad News was far more slapstick in its approach, sending up metal bands who live out their rock star fantasies in small, grubby pubs and clubs. Although both these bands went out on the road, these tours were never more than extensions of the celluloid joke. Both GWAR and Haunted Garage, on the other hand, were bands in their own right, and took their live shows to theatrical extremes. Perversely, GWAR later filmed their own movie, *Phallus In Wonderland*, in an attempt to bring the blood and guts of their live shows to a wider audience.

2

LIPSTICK AND LEATHER

Glam metal, hair metal, poseur metal, poodle rock, sleaze rock, cock rock, lite metal, pop metal, 'nerf metal, false metal: it's easy to pass glam metal off as a joke.

Certainly glam's existence can anger and embarrass plenty of metal fans – today, just as it did in the 80s – but here's Mötley Crüe's Vince Neil: "When Mötley Crüe came on the scene, it was less as a band than as a gang." A statement any true metaller could be proud of. Imagine Ozzy saying that about Black Sabbath? Or Cronos talking about Venom? Sounds *exactly* like something they could have said. Of course, he went on to say: "We'd get drunk, do crazy amounts of cocaine, and walk the circuit in stiletto heels, stumbling all over the place." But let's allow glam to have it's own idiosyncrasies. Let's not forget, Slayer wore make-up once.

What Vince Neil is really getting at here is that glam metal is about the time-honoured holy trinity of sex, drugs, and rock'n'roll. W.A.S.P.'s Blackie Lawless, on the live version of their controversial hit "Animal (Fuck Like A Beast)", asks the question: "Anybody come here looking for a little bit of pussy?" before gleefully listing everything he loves about women. Sexist, testosterone-fuelled, and just plain stupid, "Animal" is a perfect example of the LA rock scene's attitude to life. Perhaps it was a reaction against the swords and sorcery fixations of many of the NWOBHM (New Wave of British Heavy Metal) bands, or perhaps it was just that the American bands wanted to party. Either way, glam put the fun back into metal. There is no way in the world you can take yourself seriously (as a man *or* a woman) wearing six-inch heels, bright red lipstick, lurid green nail varnish, and tight pink spandex pants, with three cans of hairspray keeping the end of your hair a full 12 inches above your head.

On the whole, glam covers had but one area of concern: sex. Take a look at its origins and it becomes blindingly obvious. The New York Dolls reeked of it. They may have

NEW YORK DOLLS NEW YORK DOLLS 1973

dressed like women on the cover of their 1973 debut album, but it's clear that builders in drag they were not. Their influence is far reaching; from Britny Fox to Mötley Crüe, everyone wanted to be Johnny Thunders. And if they didn't want to be the New York Dolls' legendary frontman, they wanted to be Iggy Pop. Like the Dolls, Iggy was the epitome of cool. Sexy, androgenous, fucked up: a rock'n'roll prince and a hero to all. His appeal transcended musical boundaries; even David Bowie was in awe. Yet neither of these acts can be awarded the credit of giving rise to glam metal. For that, we have to turn to Boston's Aerosmith, who took the glammy image of the New York Dolls and mixed it with rock, creating the blueprint for glam metal in the process.

Flick through this chapter and you'll be hard pushed to find a cover that doesn't have some allusion to sex. As with Cinderella's *Night Songs* and Britny Fox's *Britny Fox*, it's the band members' own image that alludes to their sexual prowess, or, in the case of Ratt's *Out Of The Cellar*, it's an image of a scantily clad woman that's chosen to promote the band's sexual athleticism. And even when there isn't the slightest hint of flesh on show – Bullet Boys' eponymous debut had nothing more innocuous than an apple on it – they could still make it quite clear what they were all about.

When the "biggest band in the world", Guns n'Roses, released *Appetite For Destruction* in 1987, the cover art alone managed to offend enough people for it to be pulled promptly by their record company, who replaced it with a tame and more traditional metal cover. That first cover was an original painting (also titled "Appetite For Destruction") by Robert Williams. It showed that glam metal, or in this case, sleaze metal – Guns n'Roses' image was never really pretty boy, more completely wasted boy – had the kind of in-your-face, do-what-I-like, who-cares-what-you-think attitude that metal had been wearing on its sleeve since day one. After all, this is the record with the lines that every teenager of that generation has at one time gleefully sung along to: "I see you standing up, You think you're so cool. Why don't you just, Fuck off!"

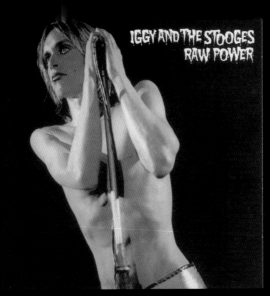

IGGY & THE STOOGES **RAW POWER** 1973

AEROSMITH **TOYS IN THE ATTIC** 1975

W.A.S.P. were the closest thing to a full-on heavy metal band the glam scene would ever produce. Their live shows involved blood drinking, meat throwing, throat slitting, hooded topless women in cages and flaming codpieces, and they were everything traditional metal fans wanted from a band, even if their album covers never reflected the blood and guts theatrics of their live shows.

At the other end of the spectrum was Poison. Lambasted for their feather-light brand of rock by the rest of the metal community, Poison still managed to get themselves a bad-boy name with the cover to *Open Up And Say... Ahh!* No doubt America's youth would be eternally warped if they were exposed to a picture of a man (or is it a woman?) dressed in a tiger-print leotard, with a prosthetic, extra-long, pointy tongue. In any event, the cover was censored until only the eyes could be seen.

What was most bizarre though, in all of this big hair madness, was Stryper. Stryper was the first band that had risen to international fame as a Christian metal band. Stryper bemused most metal fans. A band that handed out bibles instead of hurling meat into the crowd couldn't be metal, *could* they? If metal was essentially about teenage rebellion and the pursuit of the rock'n'roll myth, surely a band that promoted prayer, abstinence from premarital sex and respect for your elders was the exact antithesis to metal. But looking at the cover to their 1986 album, *To Hell With The Devil*, it's easy to see why they might, at first, attract metal fans. Four muscular, winged, long-haired men battle with a half-man, half-demon and hurl him into a fiery pit, breaking an electric guitar in the process. It's a classic metal style; if you didn't know it, you would never think these guys were Christians. And when you saw the band, clad in tight black and yellow-striped spandex and leather with enormous hairdos, like hornets with beehives, it was obvious that these guys were glam rockers too.

HANOI ROCKS

TWO STEPS FROM THE MOVE

HANOI ROCKS TWO STEPS FROM THE MOVE 1984

VOW WOW **BEAT OF METAL MOTION** 1984

TWISTED SISTER **STAY HUNGRY** 1984

MADAME X **WE RESERVE THE RIGHT** 1984

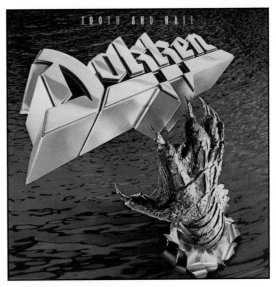

DOKKEN **TOOTH AND NAIL** 1984

MÖTLEY CRÜE

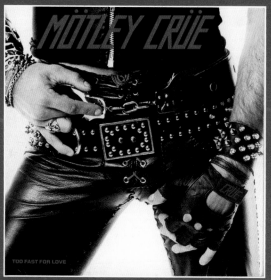

TOO FAST FOR LOVE 1982

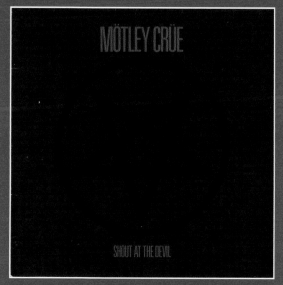

SHOUT AT THE DEVIL 1983

Guns n'Roses may have risen rapidly to the top on the basis of their debut album, but with the release of *Use Your Illusion I*, and *II*, they quickly mutated into an overblown rock behemoth. No, the real kings of glam were Mötley Crüe, a band that kept its feet planted firmly on metal terra firma whilst flying the rock'n'roll party animal flag from the highest turret. Mötley Crüe didn't stick to one theme for their covers. Their debut, *Too Fast For Love*, stunk of sex — what else could a close-up of a man's leatherbound crotch be about? Yet the original gatefold cover of the sequel, *Shout At The Devil*, was a simple black

SHOUT AT THE DEVIL inside gatefold

piece with a glossy, black pentagram in the centre, much like the satanic imagery of a Venom cover (this was quickly dropped by the record company and replaced with the inner gatefold shots of the band members). They changed tack again with their third album, *Theatre Of Pain*, using the twin masks of tragedy and comedy (note the tiny pentagram) before returning to their glam roots with 1987's *Girls Girls Girls*. *Dr Feelgood*, the last of the great Mötley Crüe albums, was straight out of the heavy metal handbook, containing the classic elements of wings, sword, skull, and serpent.

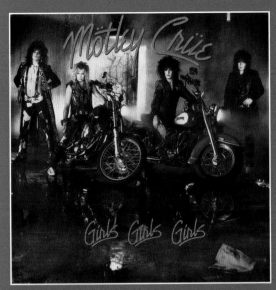

GIRLS GIRLS GIRLS 1987

GIRLS GIRLS GIRLS back cover

> *Dr Feelgood*, the last of the great Mötley Crüe albums, was straight out of the heavy metal handbook, containing the classic elements of wings, sword, skull, and serpent.

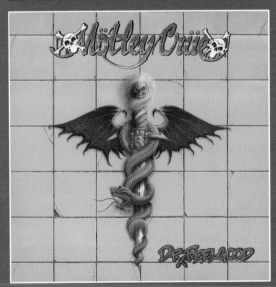

DR FEELGOOD 1989

WRATHCHILD STAKK ATTAKK 1984   W.A.S.P. **W.A.S.P.** 1984

SABU **HEARTBREAK** 1985

TWISTED SISTER COME OUT AND PLAY 1985

Pop-up of Dee Snider

66 Twisted Sister's "We're Not Gonna Take It" featured in the Parents' Music Resource Center's "Filthy Fifteen" list of most hated songs. They cited the track as too violent. Had they seen the flip-top cover to *Come Out And Play*, they may have felt differently. **99**

HEAVY PETTIN **ROCK AIN'T DEAD** 1985

STRYPER **TO HELL WITH THE DEVIL** 1986

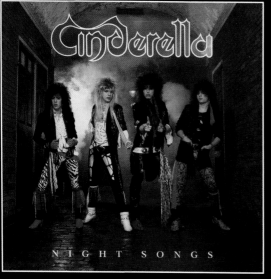

CINDERELLA **NIGHT SONGS** 1986

> **"** Even Bon Jovi courted controversy with their initial choice of album cover for *Slippery When Wet*. The wet T-shirt version was eventually released in Japan only. **"**

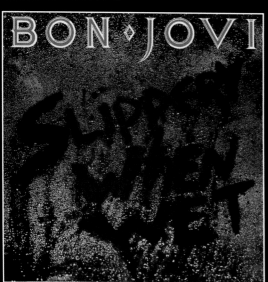

BON JOVI **SLIPPERY WHEN WET** 1986

BON JOVI **SLIPPERY WHEN WET** 1986

❝ Hanoi Rocks give fans a visual list of everything they need to be a real glam rocker. If you didn't drink Jack Daniels and smoke Marlboro reds then you just weren't glam, dude. ❞

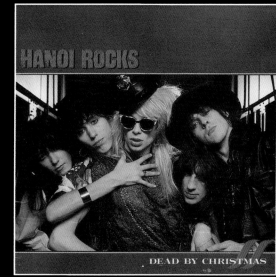

HANOI ROCKS **DEAD BY CHRISTMAS** 1986

DEAD BY CHRISTMAS Inner gatefold

GUNS N'ROSES **APPETITE FOR DESTRUCTION** 1987

GUNS N'ROSES **APPETITE FOR DESTRUCTION** 1987

WHITE LION **PRIDE** 1987

TIGERTAILZ **YOUNG AND CRAZY** 1987

FASTER PUSSYCAT **FASTER PUSSYCAT** 1987

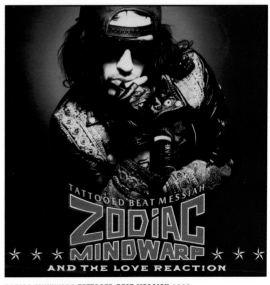

ZODIAC MINDWARP **TATTOOED BEAT MESSIAH** 1988

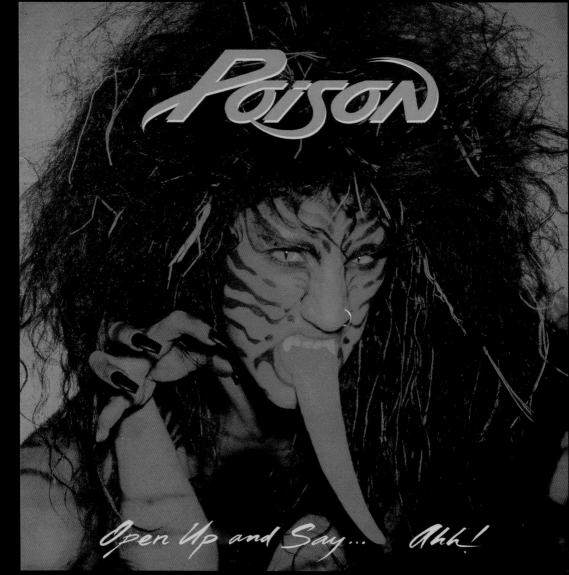

POISON OPEN UP AND SAY... AHH! 1988

BRET MICHAELS

RIKKI ROCKETT

BOBBY DALL

C.C. DEVILLE

OPEN UP AND SAY... AHH! Back cover

WINGER **WINGER** 1988

GUNS N'ROSES **GN'R LIES** 1988

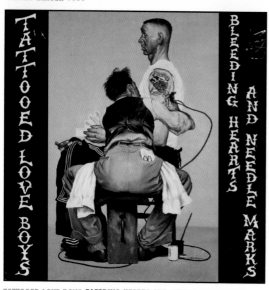

TATTOOED LOVE BOYS **BLEEDING HEARTS AND NEEDLE MARKS** 1988

BRITNY FOX **BRITNY FOX** 1988

L.A. GUNS **L.A. GUNS** 1988

SMASHED GLADYS **SOCIAL INTERCOURSE** 1988

SOHO ROSES **THE THIRD AND FINAL INSULT** 1988

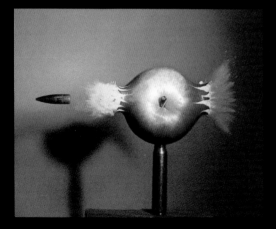

BULLET BOYS **BULLET BOYS** 1988

LITA FORD **LITA** 1988

DANGEROUS TOYS **DANGEROUS TOYS** 1988

SEA HAGS **SEA HAGS** 1988

CATS IN BOOTS **KICKED AND KLAWED** 1989

LISA DOMINIQUE **ROCK N'ROLL LADY** 1989

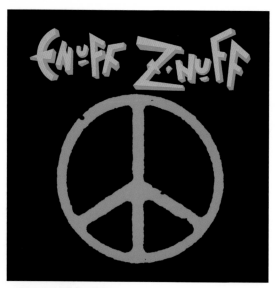

ENUFF Z'NUFF **ENUFF Z'NUFF** 1989

HORSE **LONDON** 1989

GREAT WHITE **TWICE SHY** 1989

TESLA **THE GREAT RADIO CONTROVERSY** 1989

" Glam bands were never shy of appearing on the covers of their albums. A case of you love us, we love us, so let's party! **"**

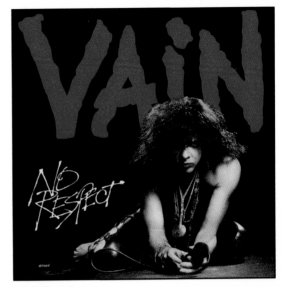

VAIN **VAIN** 1989

ELECTRIC BOYS **FUNK-O-METAL CARPET RIDE** 1990

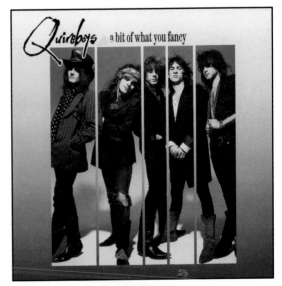

QUIREBOYS **A BIT OF WHAT YOU FANCY** 1990

TIGERTAILZ BEZERK 1990

❝ After their debut album, *Young & Crazy*, was released in 1987 with uninspiring cover art, bassist Pepsi Tate took control of design for all future Tigertailz albums.**❞**

BEZERK inner gatefold

THE DOGS D'AMOUR **STRAIGHT** 1990

SKID ROW **SLAVE TO THE GRIND** 1991

LOVE/HATE **WASTED IN AMERICA** 1992

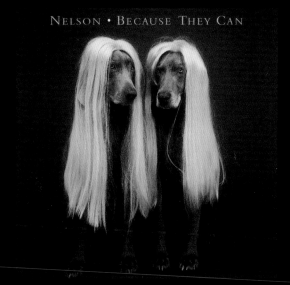

NELSON **BECAUSE THEY CAN** 1995

METAL THRASHING MAD

The New Wave Of British Heavy Metal bands and other heavy metal pioneers were never seriously troubled by glam metal. A lighter, radio-friendly version of metal was never going to be of any concern to bands like Saxon and Judas Priest.

The fact that most acts were deemed too heavy for radio was a mark of a band's credibility in metal circles.By the time Metallica released their third album you knew the game was up for both glam and heavy metal. But Metallica were not the first thrash metal band. Venom, today seen as one of the precursors to the black metal movement, were at the time considered thrash metal progenitors – to a degree, that's what they played, albeit a more abrasive, spiky kind, steeped in satanic imagery. Venom were amongst the first bands to play up to the devil-worshipper tag metal bands had earned. Their debut album, 1981's *Welcome to Hell*, went straight for the jugular, a horned goat's head inside a pentagram. Simple and effective, variations on this classic satanic symbol have adorned metal albums ever since. Their second effort, 1982's *Black Metal*, is acknowledged as the first known use of the term. They followed it with a masterpiece in satanic album cover art: *At War With Satan* (1983) was released as a gatefold satanic bible, "The Book Of Armageddon", which miraculously managed to avoid censorship. But what they were doing with the cover of *Possessed* from 1985 is anybody's guess...

Thrash metal's influences weren't all metal. The power and speed of many American hardcore punk bands reflected thrash metal's own aggressive style to such an extent that gradually a new style emerged: hardcore/thrash crossover. Corrosion Of Conformity's cult classic *Eye For An Eye* from 1982 is an early example of the style, recognized today as the first real crossover album. There were plenty of albums to draw

your attention to this new, faster, heavier style of music: Anthrax's *Fistful Of Metal* (1984), Exodus' *Bonded By Blood* (1985), and S.O.D.'s legendary *Speak English Or Die* (1985), an album, album cover, and even band inspired by a right-wing cartoon character, Sergeant D, drawn by Anthrax/S.O.D. drummer, Charlie Benante. But, despite the efforts of these furious thrashers, Metallica spelled disaster for thrash metal's predecessors – though it wasn't until 1986's *Master Of Puppets* that the final nail in heavy metal's coffin was driven in.

No sooner had you put the record on than "Battery" was kicking you smack in the throat. By the time it finished, a full five minutes and ten seconds later, your heart was beating so fast it left a dent in your chest, you'd taken up playing guitar, and your neck had been replaced by a tightly wound steel spring. In short, you'd been converted.

Once you'd been bitten by the bug, there was no going back. Heavy metal just wasn't heavy enough, and *glam*? Well, how could you carry on listening to the Tattooed Love Boys after you'd heard S.O.D.'s "Milano Mosh"?

You think you're really hard, you think that you can mosh,
Got your suspenders and got your boots,
Better wear armour, you fuckin' tool,
We mosh until you die, we mosh until you fry!

Whereas at one time a metal fan could have worn a Mötley Crüe T-shirt to an Iron Maiden gig, thrash metal drew a line: either you're a metal fan or you're a poseur.

The influence of the hardcore punk scene, combined with a desire to distance the genre from glam, ensured that love songs, or songs that had anything to do with the musicians' sexual prowess were out. Instead, apocalyptic themes were explored. The mushroom cloud and the bombed-out city were popular choices amongst thrash bands for cover art. Megadeth's second album, *Peace Sells... But Who's Buying?* (1986),

VENOM **BLACK METAL** 1982

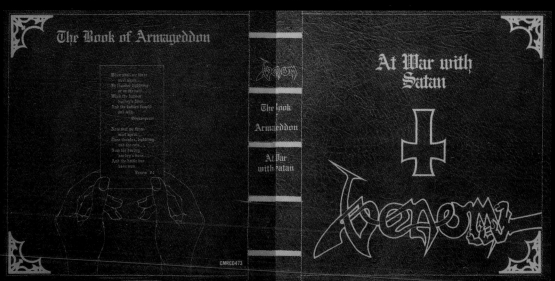

VENOM **POSSESSED** 1985

VENOM **AT WAR WITH SATAN** 1983

featured the band's mascot, Vic Rattlehead, posing as a real estate agent trying to sell a decimated UN building. Nuclear Assault consistently released albums with covers decrying a world seemingly bent on self-destruction.

Authority figures also came under fire from thrash and crossover bands. Both M.O.D., with their 1987 release, *U.S.A. For M.O.D.*, and Suicidal Tendencies, with their album from the same year, *Join The Army*, mocked Uncle Sam. Attitude Adjustment's cover for *American Paranoia* from 1986 made their view of post-Vietnam America clear.

But there was still room for classic metal covers, and monsters and demons adorned many thrash metal albums. One of the most striking fantasy art covers came from UK act, Sabbat. Sabbat used an original piece of art by recognized fantasy illustrator, John Blanche, for the cover of their 1988 album, *History Of A Time To Come*, the sales of which must surely have been boosted on the strength of the cover alone.

However, in 1985, the Swiss band Celtic Frost released an album with a cover and gatefold that outshined everything. Renowned artist HR Geiger allowed them free use of his painting, "Satan I", for the cover of *To Mega Therion*, and another, "Victory III" for the gatefold. Celtic Frost recognized the power of art to convey their image, and followed this album's success with 1987's *Into The Pandemonium*, this time using a panel ("Hell") from Hieronymus Bosch's 1504 triptych "The Garden Of Earthly Delights".

All this gives the impression that thrash metal bands took themselves and their music very seriously, until you consider thrash jokers like Lawnmower Deth, who could always be relied upon to behave like hairy clowns, and proud beer-guzzling loons Tankard and Gang Green, who wrote more paeons to beer drinking than anything else.

Finally, we cannot talk about thrash metal album covers and fail to mention Pantera's 1992 classic *A Vulgar Display Of Power*, for which it is reputed that a fan allowed the band members to punch him in the face over 80 times until they got the required shot for the cover. Metal fans: they're a dedicated lot.

CORROSION OF CONFORMITY **EYE FOR AN EYE** 1982

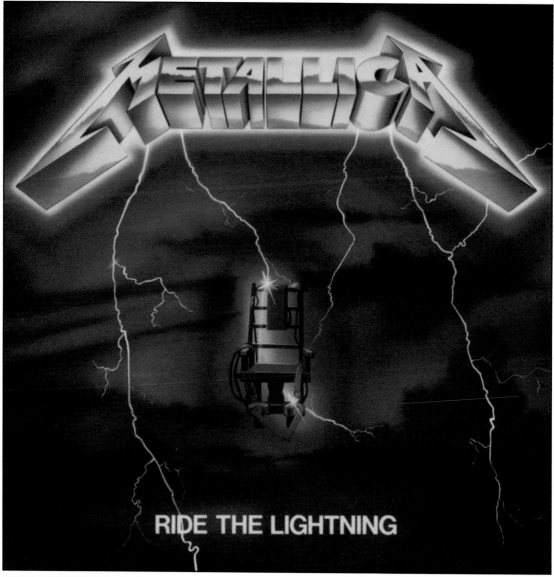

ANTHRAX **A FISTFUL OF METAL** 1984

S.O.D. **SPEAK ENGLISH OR DIE** 1985

ONSLAUGHT **POWER FROM HELL** 1985

RAZOR **EVIL INVADERS** 1985

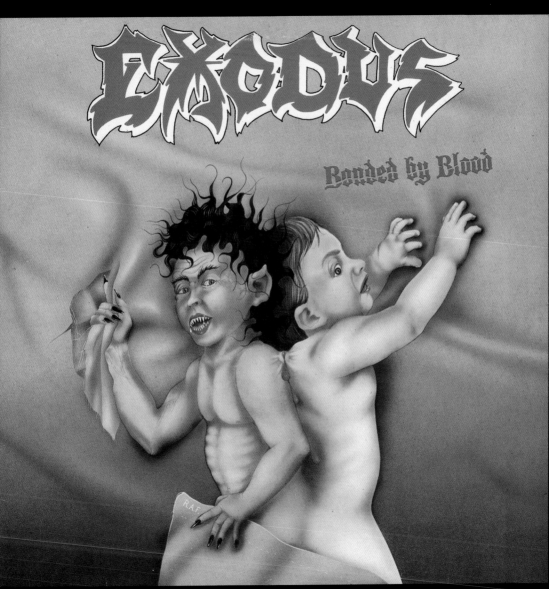

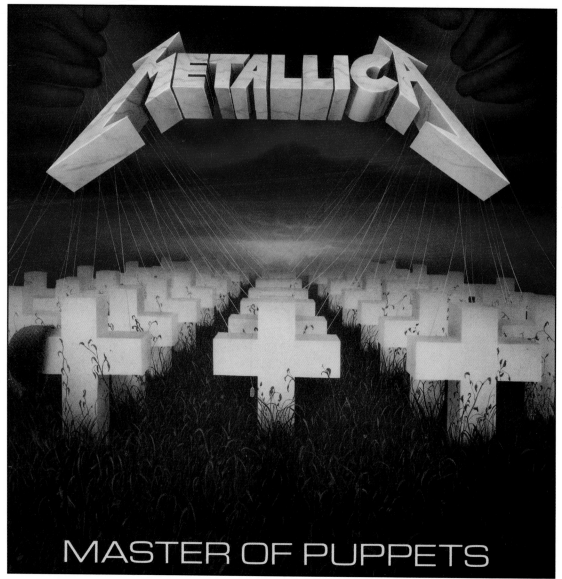

MEGADETH **PEACE SELLS... BUT WHO'S BUYING?** 1986

NUCLEAR ASSAULT **GAME OVER** 1986

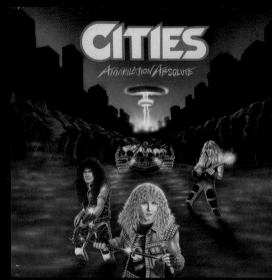

CITIES **ANNIHILATION ABSOLUTE** 1986

VOIVOD **RROOAAR** 1986

ATTITUDE ADJUSTMENT **AMERICAN PARANOIA** 1986

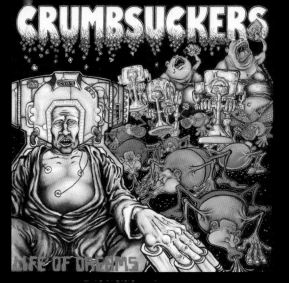

CRUMBSUCKERS

Life of Dreams

FLOTSAM AND JETSAM

DOOMSDAY FOR THE DECEIVER

CELTIC FROST TO MEGA THERION 1985

> " Swiss band Celtic Frost released an album with a cover and gatefold that outshined everything. Renouned artist HR Geiger allowed them free use of two of his paintings for *To Mega Therion*. "

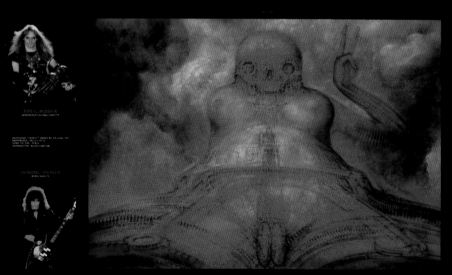

TO MEGA THERION inside gatefold

CELTIC FROST **INTO THE PANDEMONIUM** 1987

INTO THE PANDEMONIUM inside gatefold

VOIVOD **KILLING TECHNOLOGY** 1987

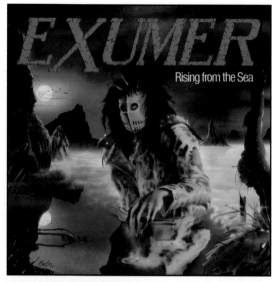

EXUMER **RISING FROM THE SEA** 1987

CIVILISED SOCIETY? **VIOLENCE SUCKS!** 1987

OVERKILL **TAKING OVER** 1987

M.O.D. **U.S.A. FOR M.O.D.** 1987

SUICIDAL TENDENCIES **JOIN THE ARMY** 1987

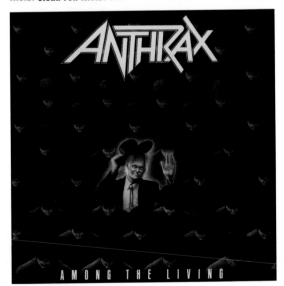

ANTHRAX **AMONG THE LIVING** 1987

CARNIVORE **RETALIATION** 1987

KREATOR

ENDLESS PAIN 1985

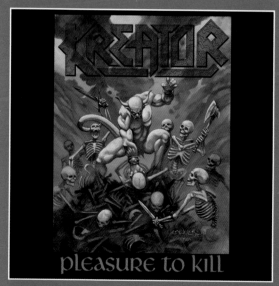

PLEASURE TO KILL 1986

You could always rely on German thrash giants Kreator to embody the characteristics of thrash metal: their album covers are amongst the finest examples of the genre.

Pleasure To Kill (1986) grabs you by your lower jaw and yanks you right in. Painted in red, black, and white and framed by two bands of thick solid black, the one-sided battle between a muscle-bound, omnipotent horned demon and a horde of overwhelmed, living-skeleton warriors challenges you to ignore this seminal record at your peril. Likewise,

OUT OF THE DARK... INTO THE LIGHT 1988

COMA OF SOULS 1990

their 1998 EP *Out Of The Dark... Into the Light* employs the same red, black, and white motif to equally compelling effect.

Like Celtic Frost before them, Kreator looked to Hieronymus Bosch for their 1990 album *Coma Of Souls* when they took part of his 16th century triptych *The Last Judgement* for their cover art.

Even Kreator's logo screamed metal at you, heavily influenced as it was by Iron Maiden's iconic moniker. Kreator's album covers made you want to headbang before you'd even got them out of the record store.

SACRED REICH **SURF NICARAGUA** 1988

THE ACCÜSED **HYMNS FOR THE DERANGED** 1988

M.O.D. **SURFIN' M.O.D.** 1988

ACID REIGN **"MOSHKINSTEIN"** 1988

NUCLEAR ASSAULT

SURVIVE

SABBAT **HISTORY OF A TIME TO COME** 1988

WARFARE **DEATHCHARGE** 1988

OVERKILL **!!!FUCK YOU!!!** 1988

HELLOWEEN **KEEPER OF THE SEVEN KEYS** 1988

CEREBRAL FIX **LIFE SUCKS AND THEN YOU DIE!** 1988

LAWNMOWER DETH **MOWER LIBERATION FRONT** 1989

METAL DUCK **QUACK EM ALL** 1989

SLAYER

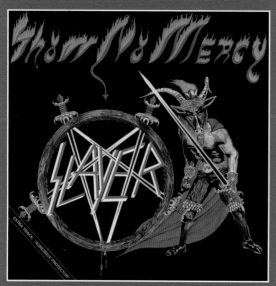

SHOW NO MERCY 1983

LIVE UNDEAD 1985

It's impossible to comprehend fully the effect that this band's 1986 release, *Reign In Blood*, had on metal fans of the time, unless you were there. Their previous covers seem immature, theatrical and cartoonish when you stand them next to this, the most cherished of all thrash albums. *Reign In Blood*'s cover is genuinely disturbing, like a glimpse into the mind of a psychopath. Every album cover before it on which Satan had ever appeared looked like it belonged on a Dungeons and Dragons game, or a horror-movie poster. *Reign In Blood* looked like the Apocalypse had finally arrived.

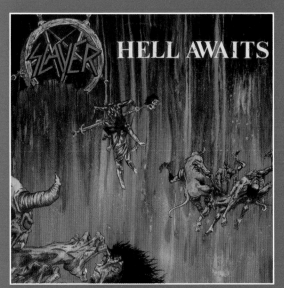

HELL AWAITS 1985

REIGN IN BLOOD 1986

Like Celtic Frost before them, Slayer stepped away from the archetypal metal album cover stereotype, employing renowned designer Steve Byram to create a cover that would compliment their ferocious and terrifying music. This choice of designer was a timely stroke of genius. *Reign In Blood* catapulted Slayer from being thrash legends to international stars, recognized kings of metal. It's clear from their previous album covers that had they not used such a skilled artist *Reign In Blood*, in appearance at least, would have been just another satanic metal album cover.

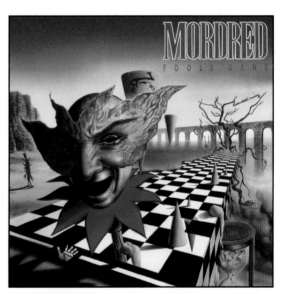

EXCEL **THE JOKE'S ON YOU** 1989

MORDRED **FOOL'S GAME** 1989

TESTAMENT SOULS OF BLACK 1990

ORANAGA **GOD'S GIFT** 1990

TANKARD **THE MEANING OF LIFE** 1990

HUMAN WRECKAGE

R.A.M. **HUMAN WRECKAGE** 1990

THE AMERICAN WAY

SACRED REICH **THE AMERICAN WAY** 1990

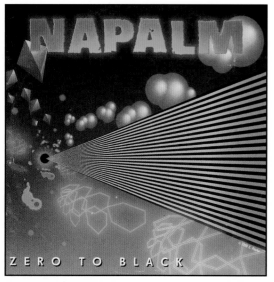

NAPALM **ZERO TO BLACK** 1990

ACID REIGN **OBNOXIOUS** 1990

GANG GREEN **KING OF BANDS** 1991

DARK ANGEL **TIME DOES NOT HEAL** 1991

ANNIHILATOR **IN COMMAND** 1991

FORCED ENTRY **AS ABOVE SO BELOW** 1991

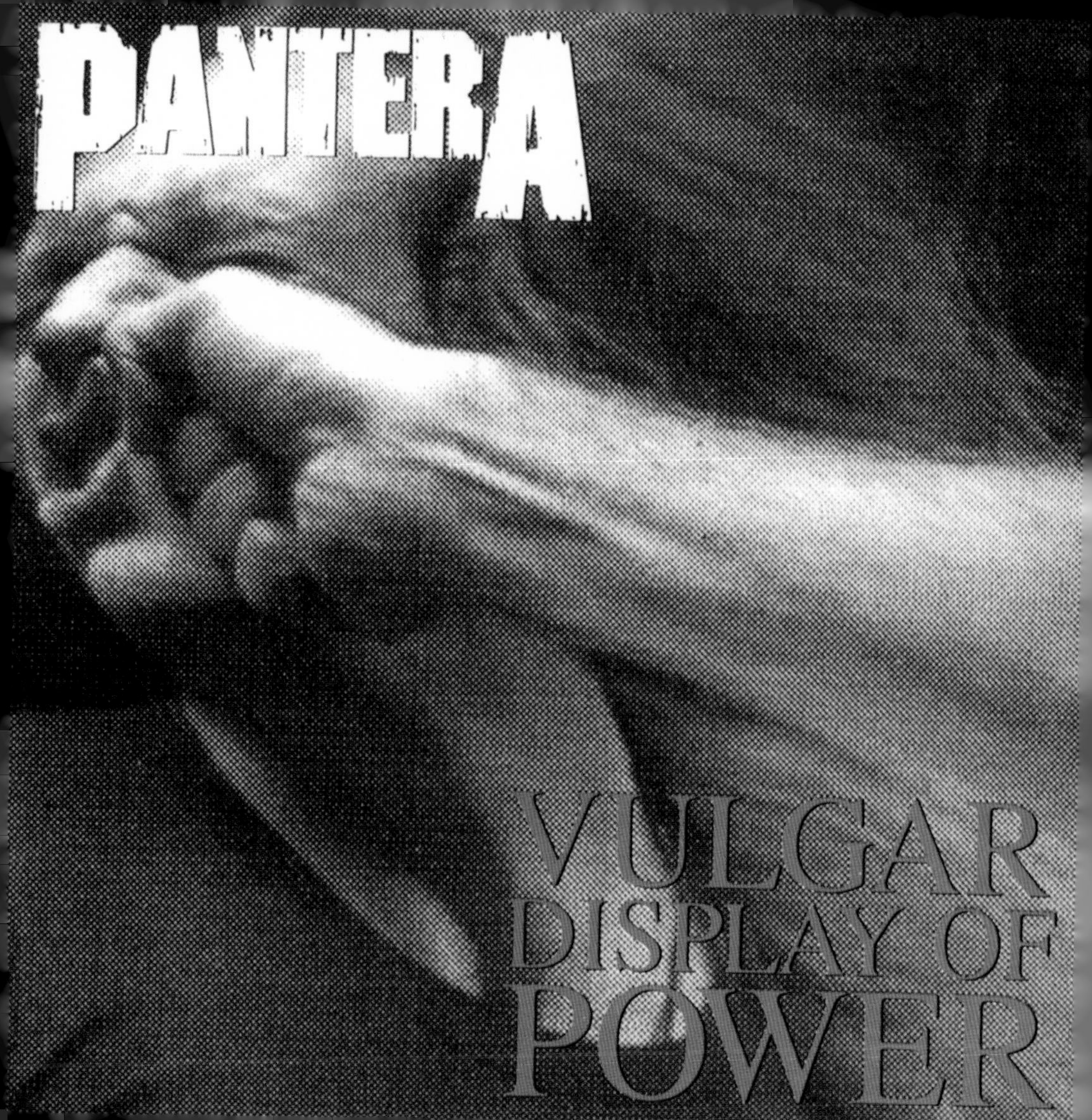
PANTERA
VULGAR DISPLAY OF POWER

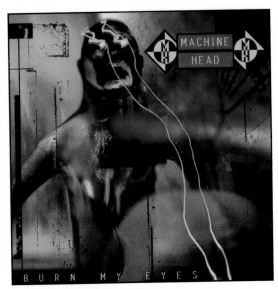

MACHINE HEAD **BURN MY EYES** 1994

GRAVE DIGGER **TUNES OF WAR** 1996

SPEED KILLS: THE VERY BEST IN SPEED METAL 1985

SPEED KILLS II: THE MAYHEM CONTINUES... 1986

SPEED KILLS III: A CATALOGUE OF DESTRUCTION 1987

HELL COMES TO YOUR HOUSE 1984

"DEREK RIGGS"

Of all the album covers within these pages, none are more instantly recognizable, nor held in such high esteem by metal fans, than those of Iron Maiden. Without exception, they will all be able to tell you who designed the covers to Iron Maiden's greatest albums: Derek Riggs, the creator of metal's most infamous mascot, Eddie The 'Ead. "The picture of Eddie that became their first album cover was a picture I did a year and a half before they ever saw it," says Riggs. "He wasn't called Eddie back then. I used to give my paintings silly titles because everyone else's were terribly meaningful. They'd paint pictures of muscular guys with swords and call them 'The Last of the Few' or something. So I had this picture of a skull thing in a T-shirt with hair sticking up – he didn't have long hair at the time, he had punky hair because it was the late 70s, the punk era. The picture was called 'Electric Matthew Says Hello'."

Riggs was thrown out of art college in Coventry for "disagreeing with them and making a nuisance of myself", just over a year into a graphic design course. He then worked as a photographic printer, spending his evenings working on illustrations before taking up album cover design.

IRON MAIDEN 1980

KILLERS 1981

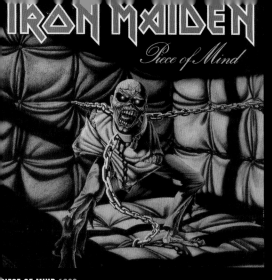

PIECE OF MIND 1983

POWERSLAVE 1984

"I just wandered around record companies with my portfolio. We're talking late 70s/early 80s, so there were just the big record companies here [in the UK]: EMI, CBS, WEA, and so forth. I sold a couple here and there. The people at EMI said they'd been there ten years and I was the first person to just walk though the door with a portfolio. The whole market was wide open. The first couple of assignments were jazz covers for EMI. They were kind of simple, a mixture of surreal and fantasy, and not very good."

Making the transition from jazz to metal was pretty simple. "Because there weren't any independent labels as such – though Led Zeppelin started their own label, which was revolutionary at the time – there wasn't really any separation between doing a jazz cover and a heavy metal cover. I did some work for a reggae band, and some private commissions – I sold a couple of pictures to Kate Bush and her family. I also did some rock and disco covers because the same art directors were doing everything."

But it wasn't until his work came to the attention of Iron Maiden's management that Riggs was able to quit dragging his portfolio around town. "The art director at EMI had some of my work on his wall and Rod Smallwood, Iron Maiden's manager, saw them and liked them. He was looking for an artist with a strange style. He asked to see my portfolio, so I stuffed a bunch of paintings into this big, wooden portfolio and dragged it down to the recording studio where they were putting together their first album."

It was then that Iron Maiden first saw Eddie. "I got the idea from HP Lovecraft, who said it was easy to make something scary when you're in the middle of Transylvania and there's smoke and bats everywhere, but the real art of horror is to make it scary on the street you live on. I thought it was a cool idea, so I stole it. So the background is a street I used to live on in London. Iron Maiden called him Ed because they just had his head. He had the skull face and the lights in his eyes and they used just his head for the logo."

Driven by a desire to be the biggest metal band in the world, and with a manager who had a reputation for being a hardcore taskmaster, Iron Maiden toured the world almost non-stop from the moment 1982's *Number Of The Beast* hit the shelves. With a repertoire that contained some of heavy metal's greatest moments ("Number Of The Beast", "Hallowed Be Thy Name", "Running Wild"), Maiden was always destined to become a legendary band. But don't forget that Iron Maiden released their debut album at a time when there was no MTV, there was no *Kerrang!* magazine (the original heavy metal bible – a source of metal news on both sides of the Atlantic). If you wanted to find out about a band you had to buy their album. Maiden were born into the New Wave Of British Heavy Metal, a time when there were a myriad of metal bands vying for attention, but when metal fans were confronted by Riggs' album covers in record stores it was absolutely impossible for them to ignore these metal icons.

"When I did that first painting, before I met Iron Maiden, I looked at it and said, 'That's going to make me rich and famous.'"

LIVE AFTER DEATH 1985

For over ten years, Riggs helped propel Iron Maiden to the top of the pile, consistently delivering classic album cover after classic. His Eddie creation is one of the biggest-selling marketing tools any band has ever had. But such hard work at times took its toll. "With *Somewhere in Time*, I worked on that for so long, I started hallucinating. I had to stop for two weeks because I wasn't doing any work. I just sat in front of the painting, imagining where all these little characters were going and what their lives were like. They wanted it to look more *Blade Runner* than *Star Wars*, and up in the sky, I had the USS Enterprise and a few other well-known starships, and they made me take them out so they wouldn't get sued. But I stuck Batman standing on a ledge on the back sleeve. That was about three years before the *Batman* movie came out. And if you look at the front window of the building, there's a reflection of a street sign across the road that, read backwards, says, 'This is a very boring painting'. I like to stick any old rubbish in there. I managed to get Mickey Mouse in one time without getting caught. It was on the single for

SOMEWHERE IN TIME 1986

"Twilight Zone". There's a woman sitting in front of a mirror with Eddie appearing in the reflection, and behind a photo of Eddie on the dresser, Mickey Mouse is poking his head around at her. That's part of the problem with CD covers versus album covers, all those details died. It's very hard to do that sort of thing and make it visible."

Since working with Iron Maiden, Riggs has gone on to produce covers for numerous metal acts. But it is his work with Eddie the 'Ead and Iron Maiden that he will be remembered for, a body of work that will forever give the name Derek Riggs a special place in all metalheads' hearts.

4

REQUIEM FOR METAL

Like twins separated at birth, death metal and grindcore grew up on opposite sides of the Atlantic, but with the same genes. In 1985, Possessed released their debut album *Seven Churches*, and gave birth to the style of vocals that would become synonymous with the genre: the death metal grunt.

Musically speaking, *Seven Churches* was little more than a lightning-fast, thrash metal record that drew lyrical inspiration from satanism and the occult. It also contained a track titled "Death Metal", and it is from this record that the genre takes its name.

On the other side of the Atlantic, in Birmingham, England, one band was noisily honing its skills and laying waste to the UK underground scene. In 1987, Napalm Death released one of the most brutal, intense records the world had ever heard, *Scum*. And with it they created not only grindcore, a music influenced by the likes of hardcore punks Discharge, Crass, and Siege, but also the blast beat, a style of drumming that would quickly become synonymous with both death metal and grindcore. If you wanted to start your own death metal or grindcore band you had to master both the blast beat and the death metal grunt, or you'd never be taken seriously.

The covers for both *Scum* and 1988's *From Enslavement To Obliteration* are awash with political dissent and social comment, as the band railed against the greed of multinational corporations and the plight of the starving, setting the tone for future grindcore releases. However, it wasn't until Carcass, a UK grindcore band featuring ex-members of Napalm Death and grindcore legends The Electro Hippies, released *Reek Of Putrefaction* in 1988 that any real offence was caused by death metal cover art. It

shocked both critics and fans in equal measure. Carcass' members were strict vegans and vegetarians and had used a collage of autopsy photographs to register their disgust with meat-eaters.

Even today, 18 years after its release, *Reek Of Putrefaction* is still one of the most disturbing album covers in existence. The shock value of all future album covers pales in comparison. Take Cannibal Corpse's *Butchered At Birth* from 1991. In the foreground, two zombies rip an unborn foetus from its mother's body, whilst in the background numerous other foetuses hang from meat hooks. This album cover is as offensive as they come – few have been more offensive since – but next to *Reek*, it can be seen for what it really is, a simple painting of a violent, fantastical scene that could easily be at home in any of the horror movies that so heavily influenced Cannibal Corpse.

Even without provocative album covers, death metal music was brutal enough to shock most parental and religious groups. If thrash metal bands had previously raced to record the fastest, heaviest album ever, death metal had surfaced as the extreme metal genre. Any parent of a teenage death metal fan would have been horrified by the sheer sonic assault of Deicide, a band who had consistently courted controversy. Loudly acclaiming an affinity with the devil, bassist and vocalist Glen Benton branded an upside down cross into his forehead regularly. At the height of their fame, their tours and private lives were plagued by problems: religious groups protested outside performance venues; militant animal-rights activists issued bomb threats; at one point the FBI even tapped Benton's phone. Acts like Venom and Possessed had previously dabbled in satanic lyrics and imagery because it suited their music; with Deicide, it seemed as if they really meant it. *Once Upon The Cross* released in 1995 left no doubt as to the band's contempt for the Christian faith.

But for the most part, death metal bands weren't practising satanists, just metallers with a passion for extreme music. Death metal and grindcore were two kinds of music that were so brutal, the subject matter had to match.

❝ The covers for both *Scum* and *Enslavement To Obliteration* are awash with political dissent and social comment, as the band railed against the greed of multinational corporations and the plight of the starving. ❞

NAPALM DEATH **SCUM** 1987

ELECTRO HIPPIES **THE ONLY GOOD PUNK...** 1987

NAPALM DEATH **FROM ENSLAVEMENT TO OBLITERATION** 1988

There were few choices for lyrical content: in grindcore you could either take a fierce political stance, or delve into the dark recesses of the human psyche. And as for death metal, well, it was devils and demons or blood and guts. In death metal terms, the name to have on your album cover artwork credit was Dan Seagrave. Seagrave began his career as an album cover designer inadvertently when he was asked by friends in Lawnmower Deth to paint a picture for their album *Mower Liberation Front*. Then Earache, Lawnmower Deth's record company, bought another of Seagrave's paintings and used it for Morbid Angel's 1989 debut album *Altars Of Madness*. Seagrave was soon in demand, going on to produce over 20 death metal covers for a variety of bands and record labels.

But perhaps surprisingly, it wasn't all guts and goat horns. Like Celtic Frost before them, a few death metal bands had more cultured tastes and turned to high art for their covers. Morbid Angel, a band who made no secret of their satanism, used the Belgian artist J Delville's occult-influenced painting "Les Tresors De Satan" for the cover of their 1991 album, *Blessed Are The Sick*. French death metallers Mercyless turned to the surrealist Salvador Dali for the cover of their 1992 album *Abject Offerings*, using Dali's "Christ Of St John Of The Cross" to great effect. But it was Cryptopsy who merged high art and death metal together most effectively, when they chose Elizabeth Serani's "Herodias With The Head Of John The Baptist" for the cover of their 1996 album *None So Vile*. Herodias wanted John the Baptist dead after he had told King Herod, her then husband, that it had been wrong of him to take his brother Phillip's wife (Herodias) for his own. Later, during a party Herod held for his most high-ranking officers and noblemen, Herodias' daughter performed a dance that so delighted the king that he offered her a prize – anything up to the value of half his kingdom. The girl, having already been coached by her mother, promptly asked for the head of John the Baptist. Herod could hardly refuse in front of so many distinguished guests. John was duly beheaded and his head was delivered to the girl on a silver platter.

O.L.D. **OLD LADY DRIVERS** 1988

TERRORIZER **WORLD DOWNFALL** 1989

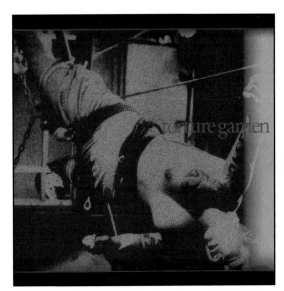

NAKED CITY **TORTURE GARDEN** 1989

SEPULTURA **BENEATH THE REMAINS** 1989

FILTHY CHRISTIANS **MEAN** 1990

INCUBUS **BEYOND THE UNKNOWN** 1990

SUMERIAN CRY

TIAMAT **SUMERIAN CRY** 1990

CANNIBAL CORPSE **EATEN BACK TO LIFE** 1990

CANNIBAL CORPSE BUTCHERED AT BIRTH 1991

DEATH

SCREAM BLOODY GORE 1987

LEPROSY 1988

It seems only right that the band that released the first true death metal record should have the moniker "Death". *Scream Bloody Gore* hit the shelves in 1987, shortly after Napalm Death's *Scum*, and although Possessed had coined the term "death metal" two years earlier, it was *Scream Bloody Gore* that gave it real meaning. Death progressed rapidly, both in terms of musical style, technical ability and with their album covers. *Scream* is an archetypal metal album cover and its follow up, *Leprosy*, does little to stray away from the formula, great though it is.

SPIRITUAL HEALING 1990

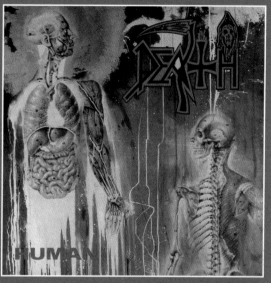
HUMAN 1991

Spiritual Healing, released in 1990, showed just how far the band had come. To the casual observer this is yet another cover decrying the Christian faith, nothing new in that. However, unlike the rest of the death metal scene, Death had walked away from gore and satanism on *Spiritual Healing*, and had turned their eye to a more topical subject. By the time Death released *Human* in 1991, they had shed the lyrical props used by their peers, with vocalist Chuck Schuldiner turning his attention inward onto himself and all humanity. The original death metal band had come of age.

PAIN KILLER BURIED SECRETS 1991

CANCER **DEATH SHALL RISE** 1991

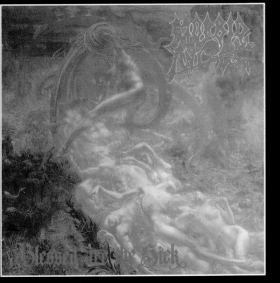

MORBID ANGEL BLESSED ARE THE SICK 1991

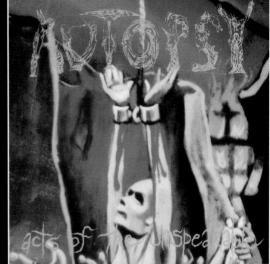

AUTOPSY ACTS OF THE UNSPEAKABLE 1992

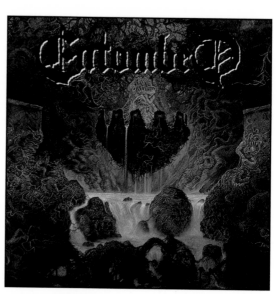

ARMOURED ANGEL **STIGMARTYR** 1992

ENTOMBED **CLANDESTINE** 1992

MALEVOLENT CREATION **RETRIBUTION** 1992

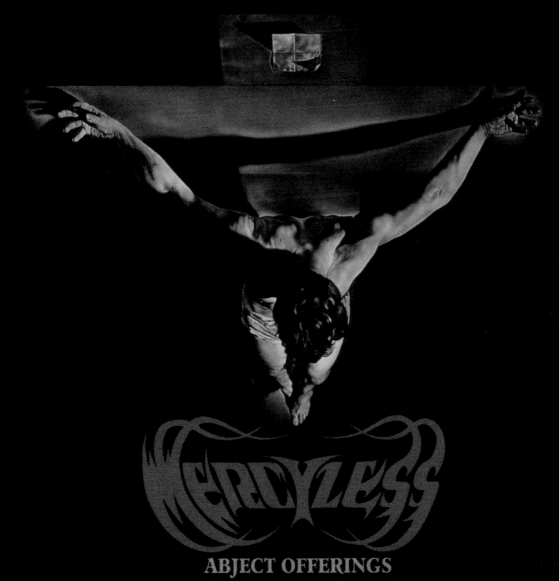

MORGOTH

ODIUM

OBITUARY

SLOWLY WE ROT 1989

CAUSE OF DEATH 1990

Obituary's 1989 debut, *Slowly We Rot*, is a classic death metal album, with a classic death metal cover. Its simplicity – a rotting corpse in the gutter, its bodily fluids leaking into a drain – coupled with the album's title fill the viewer's head with morbid thoughts. Which is exactly the kind of reaction death metal bands sought to provoke. *Slowly We Rot* has one of those covers that is so compelling you just have to buy the album, even if you've never heard of the band, and the 1990 follow-up, *Cause Of Death*, though by no means simplistic, is every bit as compelling.

THE END COMPLETE 1992

WORLD DEMISE 1994

By the time of *The End Complete* in 1992, Obituary's status as death metal heavyweights was secure, though with this album cover they lost their edge, producing little more than the standard fare. When 1994's *World Demise* was released it came with a cover that deviated from the death metal norm. Here was a band that had started out with songs that had few lyrics – frontman John Tardy preferred to vocalize grunts that fitted the music when he couldn't think of a lyric – but had now matured to tackling international environmental issues. The world of gore had long lost its appeal.

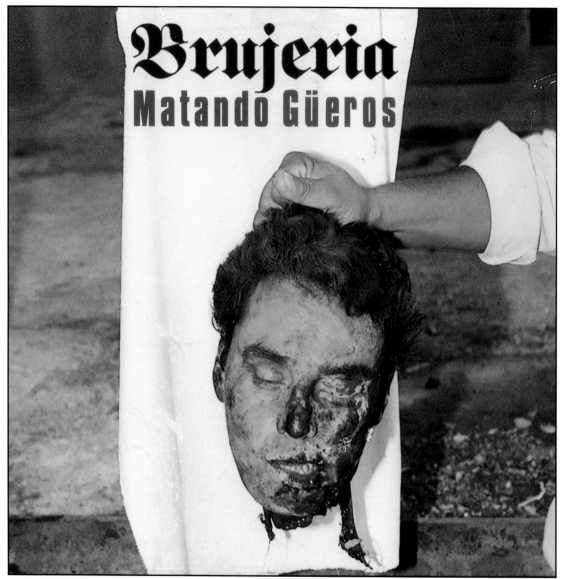

BRUJERIA **MATANDOS GÜEROS** 1993

PESTILENCE **SPHERES** 1993

SADISTIK EXEKUTION **WE ARE DEATH FUKK YOU** 1994

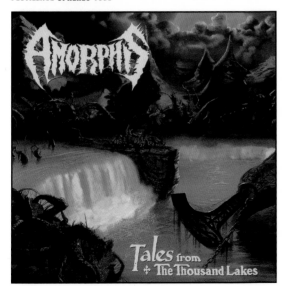

AMORPHIS **TALES FROM THE THOUSAND LAKES** 1994

KONKHRA **SPIT OR SWALLOW** 1994

...FOR VICTORY

brutal truth
need to control

VADER SOTHIS 1994

OPPRESSOR SOLSTICE OF OPPRESSION 1994

DESULTORY **BITTERNESS** 1994

SIEGE **DROP DEAD** 1994

AT THE GATES SLAUGHTER OF THE SOUL 1995

SINISTER HATE 1995

DISMEMBER MASSIVE KILLING CAPACITY 1995

CRYPTOPSY **NONE SO VILE** 1996

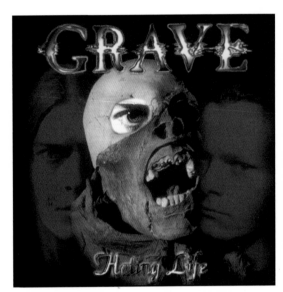

GRAVE **HATING LIFE** 1996

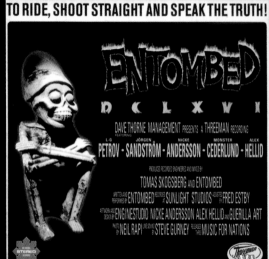

DEMILICH **NESPITHE** 1996

ENTOMBED **TO RIDE, SHOOT STRAIGHT AND SPEAK THE TRUTH!** 1997

THERION A'ARAB ZARAQ LUCID DREAMING 1997

GOLGOTHA **ELEMENTAL CHANGES** 1998

OPETH **STILL LIFE** 1999

ANGELCORPSE **THE INEXORABLE** 1999

DEFILED **ERUPTED WRATH** 1999

5

FUCK YOU, I WON'T DO WHAT YOU TELL ME

Although Nirvana are widely credited as the band that changed the face of rock, in metal terms things had been changing before Nirvana had even signed a record deal.

In Los Angeles, the Red Hot Chili Peppers, Faith No More and Jane's Addiction were joyously putting the boot into 80s glam, taking the "party-on, dude" ethos of hair metal and turning it on its head.

Of the three, Jane's Addiction's sound was closest to contemporary metal. Taking the raw, overdriven guitar sound beloved by all metal fans, Jane's Addiction blended a variety of rhythmical styles and influences. They created a unique sound all of their own that was instantly recognizable due to the distinctive vocals of their frontman, the provocative Perry Farrell. Farrell is one of music's most celebrated bohemians, oozing the kind of androgynous cool that David Bowie and Iggy Pop were born with. With him on vocals, Jane's Addiction's gigs were like freak shows. *Nothing's Shocking* released in 1988 brought Jane's Addiction to the attention of American conservative groups, who could always be relied upon to take offence at the sight of a naked woman. So when they were confronted with the sight of two naked women, joined at the hip and shoulder, with their heads on fire, they nearly choked on it and demanded that the record company pull the album and that shops stop stocking it. Thankfully, everyone concerned ignored them.

Aside from this minor scuffle, the cover to *Nothing's Shocking* is remarkable because here was an LA-based metal band using on their album cover an image of the naked female form that was neither degrading nor sexist. Though you may have found the band members hanging out with strippers and prostitutes, these women were not sex toys or conquests to be boasted about in song, as many glam bands did, but friends with lives that were rich in lyrical inspiration. The alternative to metal started right here.

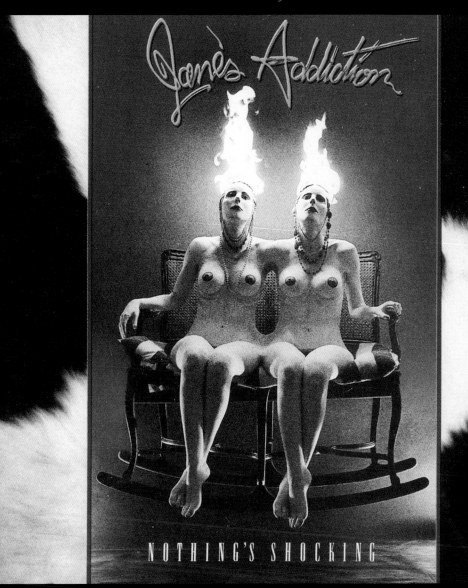

Los Angeles in the 1980s was glam rock central, but by the end of the decade the city that had given us Mötley Crüe and Guns n'Roses had turned its back on big hair and was embracing new musical cultures. Faith No More, like Jane's Addiction, was a band that had plenty of rock'n'roll spirit, but without the transvestite dress sense and mindless sexism that pervaded glam. By the time they released *The Real Thing* in 1989, they already had a reputation as an off-the-wall art rock band with a taste for metal guitar riffs and funk-influenced bass lines – the kind of band whose music you could stick on at a party and either throw yourself around to with wild abandon or stand in the kitchen drunkenly analyzing into the small hours.

The Real Thing threw this one-time cult band onto the world stage almost overnight. Heavier than anything they'd released before, *The Real Thing* was a revelation in metal terms, drawing influences from all types of music, and proving that you could play metal with keyboards and synths, something previously considered sacrilegious. The album's cover is now a recognized icon: a graphic design classic. At the time of its release, *The Real Thing* looked unlike any other metal cover: design here takes precedence over the musical branding that was typical of previous covers. It would be difficult to know exactly what kind of music to expect from this album if you didn't know the band already. Faith No More delighted in defying the critics, refusing to be cast in any genre-specific mould. Their album covers reflected this, and never more successfully than in *The Real Thing*.

It wasn't enough that LA spawned two of the most influential and original metal acts of the 90s. When the Red Hot Chili Peppers broke worldwide with their fifth studio album in 1991, *Blood, Sugar, Sex, Magik*, they brought a huge dose of funk to the party. The Chili Peppers was the ultimate party band, with a desire to do anything that was entertaining, regularly appearing on stage during encores wearing nothing but strategically placed socks over their genitals. What's more, the Chili Peppers reeked of sex, even more so than their glam metal counterparts. However, unlike glam bands, their

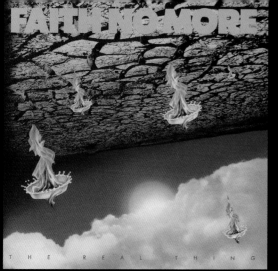

FAITH NO MORE

THE REAL THING

RED BLOOD

PEPPERS MAGIK

HOT SUGAR

CHILI-SEX

use of funky bass lines offered a more booty-shaking, grinding sexual rhythm that both sexes could get down to. Like Faith No More's *The Real Thing*, *Blood, Sugar, Sex, Magik* owes more to graphic design than heavy metal posturing.

Although these three acts gave metal fans a real alternative to glam and heavy metal, it wasn't until Nirvana released their second album, 1991's *Nevermind*, that a scene was born. No one can argue that Nirvana was ever a metal band, but it cannot be denied that without this album glam metal would still be alive today.

Nirvana spawned a thousand copycat bands. Record companies started to look to other types of music, and as a result a genre wasn't so much born as cobbled together. The bands had little in common musically, other than heavy guitars and a nod to a heavy metal influence. Their album covers reflected this right from the start. Evil monsters, demons, swords: none of them made an appearance. Perhaps the only recurring theme is that the bands distanced themselves from classic metal album cover concepts. Tool, for example, were undeniably a metal band, but you'd never know it from their album covers. Of all their covers, *Undertow* in 1993 comes closest, using only red and black, two of metal's favourite colours, but that's as far as it goes. Apart from the suggestive title, implying a pulling down into the depths, reinforced by the red-tentacled object, there's no decipherable message in this image, nor recognizable genre allegiance. Even so, Wal-Mart saw something objectionable and promptly slapped a huge barcode sticker over every copy in their stores.

But sometimes it was hard to get away from metal values. Rage Against The Machine's 1992 self-titled debut used a photograph of Thich Quang Duc, a Buddhist monk committing self-immolation in protest against Vietnamese prime minister Ngo Dinh Diem's measures against the Buddhist religion. Although it could never be said that metal had a history of protest, the anti-establishment stance of both Quang Duc and Rage Against The Machine was something that metal fans could easily relate to.

NIRVANA **NEVERMIND** 1991

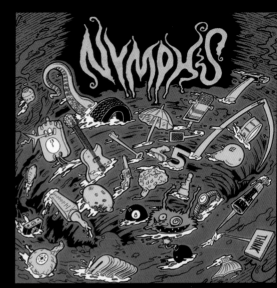

NYMPHS **NYMPHS** 1991

SOUNDGARDEN **BADMOTORFINGER** 1991

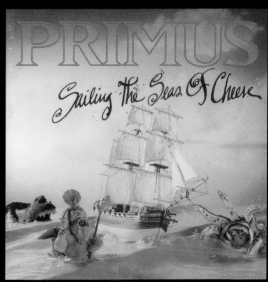

PRIMUS **SAILING THE SEAS OF CHEESE** 1991

RAGE AGAINST THE MACHINE **RAGE AGAINST THE MACHINE** 1992

HELMET MEANTIME 1992

L7 BRICKS ARE HEAVY 1992

MINISTRY PSALM 69 1992

WHITE ZOMBIE LA SEXORCISTO 1992

BODY COUNT **BODY COUNT** 1992

MINDFUNK **DROPPED** 1993

SKIN YARD **INSIDE THE EYE** 1993

TOOL **UNDERTOW** 1993

MY SISTER'S MACHINE **WALLFLOWER** 1993

NUDESWIRL **NUDESWIRL** 1993

MELVINS **HOUDINI** 1993

TYPE O NEGATIVE **THE ORIGIN OF THE FECES** 1994

STONE TEMPLE PILOTS **PURPLE** 1994

NINE INCH NAILS **THE DOWNWARD SPIRAL** 1994

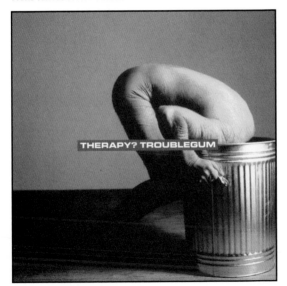

THERAPY? **TROUBLEGUM** 1994

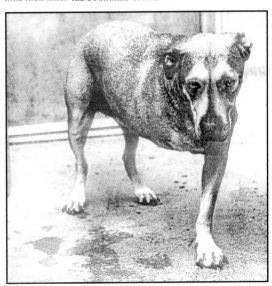

ALICE IN CHAINS **ALICE IN CHAINS** 1995

6

BLACKENED IS THE END,
WINTER IT WILL SEND

Ever since Black Sabbath had chosen such an unholy name, metal bands had toyed with satanism and the occult. Metal's subversive streak was wide enough for its bands to thrive on the notoriety that satanic imagery and songs in praise of Beelzebub bought them.

But in reality few bands that talked the talk walked the walk. The 80s English thrashers, Venom, the band that gave black metal its name, revelled in the bad-boy reputation that their satanic image lent them, but behind closed doors they were no more satanists than they were born-again Christians.

Venom's imagery, both on their album covers and in the way they dressed, heavily influenced 90s black metal, but it was Bathory that truly defined the genre. Bathory, the brainchild of one Tomas Forsberg, otherwise known as Quorthon, released their first album, *Bathory*, way back in 1984. The classic goat's head that appeared on the cover gave a clear warning of Bathory's manifesto, but the raw, aggressive music contained inside was unlike anything that had come before. The landmark album *Under The Sign Of The Black Mark* was released in 1987, with a cover that is classic metal – a monstrous, muscular beast takes centre stage – with a black metal twist – the beast is Satan himself. Rather than have him slaughtering innocents, here he is slightly romanticized by his setting: a lonely entity atop a rocky mountain ridge.

Quorthon went from producing albums that were the blueprint for all future black metal releases to creating a second, more obscure metal genre, Viking metal, with the release of *Blood, Fire, Death* in 1989. *Blood, Fire, Death* was more symphonic than his

BATHORY **BATHORY** 1984

BATHORY **THE RETURN** 1985

BATHORY **UNDER THE SIGN OF THE BLACK MARK** 1987

BATHORY **BLOOD, FIRE, DEATH** 1989

earlier musical releases, and saw Quorthon abandon Satan in favour of the Nordic god Odin. *Blood, Fire, Death*'s cover embraces Norse mythology and marked a turning point in the now one-man band's career.

But by this time, the first unashamedly, out-and-out black metal band, Norway's Mayhem, had already formed and released their debut mini-album, *Deathcrush* in 1987. Limited to a mere 1000 copies, *Deathcrush* was an instant hit on the underground scene and propelled the band's members to cult status overnight. From this band came black metal's most infamous figures, Øystein Aarseth and Varg Vikerness, known to their fans as Euronymous and Count Grishnach. Aarseth's murder at the hands of Vikerness is well documented. This cold-blooded killing, along with the suicide of vocalist Per Yngve Ohlin (aka Dead) – which had been captured on film and was used as part of the artwork for subsequent releases – and the murder of Magne Andreassen by Emperor's drummer, Bård Eithun (also known as Faust) in a Lillehammer park brought black metal to the attention of the world's press.

It appeared that the years of merely toying with dark imagery were over. Homicide, satanism and a sinister inner circle reputed to be behind a spate of church burnings combined to shroud black metal in mystery. This mysteriousness is exploited to the full by the scene's progenitors and is part of the attraction for its fans.

Looking at the album covers, it is clear that there is a certain amount of gothic romanticism involved in black metal artwork. Misty mountain peaks, spectral woodland scenes, and snow-covered landscapes are regularly used for cover material to convey a sense of the ethereal. Black metal bands identified themselves by daubing their faces with corpse paint and appearing as furious, diabolical evil-doers. Black metal, perhaps even more so than glam metal, is a musical scene that takes its image very seriously. As a result, its album covers at times are both poetic and seductive. Carpathian Forest's 1995 release, *Through Chasm, Caves And Titan Woods*, is a perfect example. The haunting

beauty of nature is marred by the sinister ambience of the shadowy building atop the plateau. Gehenna's *The First Spell* from 1994 is another album cover that avoids all the traditional metal cover concepts. Two hooded figures meet at dusk on the edge of a wood. On the one hand, this could easily be a romantic scenario, the meeting of two lovers. On the other hand, these two unidentifiable figures could be up to something far more sinister than a secret liaison.

Of course, it's not all mystery and gothic romance. Sometimes, as with Abigor's 1997 opus, *Apokalypse* and Dodheimsgard's 1996 release, *Monumental Possession*, it's good to get back to basics and slap a good old-fashioned satanic horned goat trapped in a five-pointed star on the cover. Black metal didn't always avoid metal clichés. Australia's Destroyer 666 revived that favourite image of thrash metal, the mushroom cloud, for the cover to their 1995 album, *Violence Is The Prince Of This World*. Satryicon's cover to their 1994 release *Dark Medieval Times* could be straight out of the NWOBHM.

But black metal bands did update and invigorate the tired metal image of the sword-wielding maniac by placing themselves on their covers, hidden in the shadows, wielding all kinds of weapons and adorned in cloaks, hoods and spiked armour, hiding their identities with corpse paint masks. Sometimes their attempts to appear fearsome worked, as with Darkthrone's early output, and at other times, the effect was far too comical (see Immortal's *Battles In The North*, 1995).

Perhaps the album cover that most captures the essence of black metal is Emperor's 1997 release, *Reverence*. Lose the kneeling, armed figure in the foreground and you are left with an atmospheric snow-covered landscape, a snapshot of ethereal natural beauty. The addition of a shadowed, sword-wielding man gives the cover just the right balance of menace and beauty to render it extremely arresting and seductive. On the whole, black metal's album covers are thoroughly enticing: like the forbidden fruit, they're hard to resist.

ACHERON **RITES OF THE BLACK MASS** 1991

MAYHEM **LIVE IN LEIPZIG** 1992

IMMORTAL **DIABOLICAL FULLMOON MYSTICISM** 1992

IMPALED NAZARENE **TOL COMPT NORZE, NORZE, NORZE** 1993

EMPEROR EMPEROR 1993

ABSU **BARATHRUM: V.I.T.R.I.O.L.** 1993

IMMORTAL **PURE HOLOCAUST** 1993

BURZUM

BURZUM 1993

DET SOM ENGANG VAR 1994

Perversely for black metal's most famous, or notorious son, Varg Vikerness, otherwise known as Count Grishnach, the album covers for his solo project, Burzum, contain scant reference to Satan. Only *Det Som Engang Var*, released in 1994, displays any hint of satanic imagery with its row of horned demon's heads ranged over a menacing gateway. Yet Burzum's album covers are all highly influential black metal classics. They're not issued in black and white to minimize on production costs, but to maximize the atmospheric undertones.

HVIS LYSET TAR OSS 1994

FILOSOFEM 1996

The 1993 self-titled debut album, *Burzum*, though amateurish in technique, is one of the first albums to represent the mythology of a pre-Christian Norway, a country whose folklore was awash with tales of evil characters loose in the woods. Vikerness would, like Quorthon before him, turn his back on traditional satanism entirely and dedicate himself to Odin and his homeland's folklore, returning time and again to the rich pickings therein for covers like 1994's *Hvis Lyset Tar Oss* and 1996's *Filosofem*, written and recorded in jail whilst serving a life sentence for murder.

GEHENNA **FIRST SPELL** 1994

SATYRICON **DARK MEDIEVAL TIMES** 1994

EMPEROR **IN THE NIGHTSIDE ECLIPSE** 1994

" Black metal took traditional satanic metal cover art and injected it with a dark, gothic romanticism**"**

ISENGARD **VINTERSKUGGE** 1994

ULVER **KVELDSSANGER** 1995

CARPATHIAN FOREST **THROUGH CHASM, CAVES AND TITAN WOODS** 1995

ᛒATTLES IN THE NORTH

RTH 1995

DARKTHRONE

SOULSIDE JOURNEY 1991

A BLAZE IN THE NORTHERN SKY 1991

Darkthrone began life as a typical death metal band, with the release of *Soulside Journey* in 1991. But they quickly switched to black metal, adorning themselves with the de rigeur corpse paint and releasing the uncompromisingly raw *A Blaze In The Northern Sky* that same year.

The cover to *Blaze* is a landmark moment in black metal; with this album cover Darkthrone became the first band to boldly advertise their predilection for face painting, forcing fans of metal to decide are you a black metaller or not? There was no sitting on the fence in black metal; either you

UNDER A FUNERAL MOON 1993

TRANSILVANIAN HUNGER 1994

painted your face or you didn't exist. Together with *Under A Funeral Moon*, released in 1993, Darkthrone created the classic black metal album-cover style, adjusting the contrast levels in the photographs to such a degree that only the whitest parts of the image could be seen. This toying with the colour saturation produced album covers that present the band as unholy, satanic maniacs, more demon than human. *A Blaze In The Northern Sky* spawned numerous copycat covers, but none of them had the same impact as these early Darkthrone efforts.

BEHEMOTH SVENTEVITH (STORMING NEAR THE BALTIC) 1995

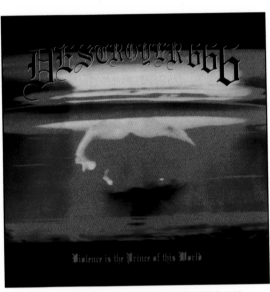

DESTROYER 666 VIOLENCE IS THE PRINCE OF THIS WORLD 1995

DIMMU BORGIR **STORMBLÅST** 1996

DODHEIMSGARD **MONUMENTAL POSSESSION** 1996

ABIGOR APOKALYPSE 1997   **EMPEROR REVERENCE** 1997

ARCTURUS **LA MASQUERADE INFERNALE** 1997

EMPEROR **ANTHEMS TO THE WELKIN AT DUSK** 1997

NOKTURNAL MORTUM **GOAT HORNS** 1997

ENTHRONED **TOWARDS THE SKULLTHRONE OF SATAN** 1997

SACRAMENTUM **THE COMING OF CHAOS** 1997

ENSLAVED **BLODHEMN** 1998

GORGOROTH DESTROYER 1998

SIEBENBURGEN GRIMJAUR 1998

THY SERPENT **CHRISTCRUSHER** 1998

MARDUK **PANZER DIVISION MARDUK** 1999

DARK FUNERAL **IN THE SIGN** 2000

7

FAIRIES WEAR BOOTS

Heavy metal is beer music. Beer and metal go together like Jack Daniels and Coke. Heaven and Hell. Or meat and potatoes. The perfect mix, one complementing the other.

This rabble-rousing liquid has bonded metal fans across the world for years, their bellies full of brew as they punch the air, scream the lyrics, and swill more beer. This was party music, rocking out music, fast music. Then metal discovered marijuana, and everything went slow.

Of course, like everything in heavy metal it seems, Black Sabbath did it first. The slow, foreboding nature of their sonic assault was so obviously influenced by the THC coursing through their veins and they weren't shy about it:

> When I first met you, didn't realize,
> I can't forget you or your surprise,
> You introduced me to my mind,
> And left me wanting you and your kind.
>> "Sweat Leaf" – Black Sabbath

Everything, from the coughing at the beginning of the track (guitarist Tony Iommi hacking up his lungs after a drag on a joint) to the song's blatant subject matter, proved that this was a band willing to let its illegal habits influence its music.

The founders of heavy metal also spawned the sub-genres of doom and stoner rock. From the late 70s to the mid-80s, bands such as Trouble and Saint Vitus became known as doom, while Sweden's Candlemass popularized the style; their 1986 album *Epicus Doomicus Metallicus* is considered a genre-defining classic.

TROUBLE **SKULL** 1984

PENTAGRAM **PENTAGRAM** 1985

CANDLEMASS **EPICUS DOOMICUS METALLICUS** 1986

MONSTER MAGNET 25...........TAB 1991

Despite their shared roots, there are distinct differences in the sounds of both stoner and doom metal. Although the melancholy of doom is at odds with the groovy, up-tempo stoner rock sounds of Fu Manchu or Queens Of The Stone Age, all of these bands take their cues from the brief period in rock history where the quest for new sounds and structures led groups away from the confines of the three-minute pop song format.

And none more so than Monster Magnet. They were, according to their infamous T-shirt slogan "a satanic drug thing, you wouldn't understand": equal parts psychedelic rock (Hawkwind, Pink Floyd), proto-punk (Stooges, MC5) and heavy rock (Led Zeppelin, Sabbath). Many of the doom/stoner album covers still used heavy metal imagery: monsters, men with swords, more monsters, bare breasts. Monster Magnet's 1991 epic *Spine Of God*, for instance, features the angry head of a bull complete with a double set of flesh-ripping horns, yet in the background spins a window into the band's drug-fuelled alternative universe. Drug paraphernalia circles the head of the bull stuck to the spine of God. "Centre of the universe, baby", as frontman Dave Wyndorf would often point out.

Yes, Monster Magnet were about as out there as psychedelic stoner rock got. This is the band that, according to legend, once spiked the entire audience with LSD and blew their minds into complete oblivion. Monster Magnet were the whole package. The music, the artwork, the lifestyle, everything blended into one glorious free for all of sex, drugs, rock'n'roll, free dope and fucking-in-the-streets orgy. The Monster Magnet covers featured here show them at the pinnacle of their powers. *Spine Of God*, with its hard-drug paranoia set the scene, while its follow up, 1993's *Superjudge*, sees the return of the bull looking equally pissed off and ready to drag you into its bad-trip hell. 1992's *Tab* was easily their most far out album musically, largely comprised of one very long and utterly hypnotic space rock jam. The album's artwork aped the classic space themes used on so many progressive rock albums of the 70s, an era from which Monster Magnet drew much of their influence.

" Monster Magnet were the whole package: sex, drugs, rock'n'roll, free dope, and fucking in the streets **"**

MONSTER MAGNET **SPINE OF GOD** 1991

SAINT VITUS **C.O.D.** 1992

EYEHATEGOD **TAKE AS NEEDED FOR PAIN** 1993

Pre-Queens Of The Stone Age legends Kyuss are to many as good as stoner rock gets. Their dusty desert rock jams brought a new strength to rock in the early 90s and their album art reflected the equally boundless sound of their music. 1994's *Welcome To Sky Valley* features a sunset-bleached sky above the infamous battered sign that leads into the Californian desert, which gave the album its name. ...*And The Circus Comes To Town*, released the following year, is equally vast, trading the scorched earth of the desert heat for the foreboding, frostbitten cold of winter.

Southern Californian quartet Fu Manchu incorporate a love of bikes, cars, and monster trucks into their imagery. Given that Fu Manchu are musically the most high-energy of the key stoner rock bands, it's fitting that their albums are adorned with high-speed vehicles. Long zoned-out space rock has never been a part of Fu Manchu's repertoire: they preferred instead to draw their influences from the early 80s Californian punk/hardcore scene (Circle Jerks, Black Flag), mixing high-speed explosions of energy with gigantic slabs of 60s fuzz rock guitar. Their covers reflected this zeal, all trucks, cars, and skateboards, conjuring up images of fat spliffs and roaring through the desert on your way to rip the hell out of a skate park while classic AC/DC blasts from the speakers!

Formed by ex-Napalm Death frontman and Rise Above Records honcho Lee Dorrian, UK-based rockers Cathedral utilized aspects of both the stoner and doom genres to create a Sabbath-fried hybrid that got the thumbs up from rock fans the world over. All their album covers were painted by artist Dave Patchett, whose work Lee saw in a gallery. Lee was drawn into Patchett's surrealist world and left a note asking Dave to call him. They met, and Lee asked him to do a cover that reflected the whole 70s trip the band were into. They continued this theme for all of their records, giving fans instantly recognizable covers without the use of an Iron Maiden Eddie-style character on every sleeve.

Welcome to the world of stoner rock, brothers and sisters – turn off your mind, relax, and float downstream.

MONSTER MAGNET **SUPERJUDGE** 1993

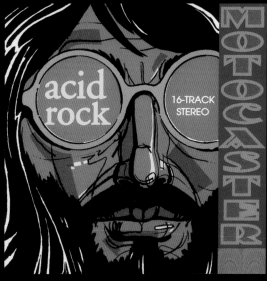

MOTORCASTER **ACID ROCK** 1994

KYUSS **WELCOME TO SKY VALLEY** 1994

KYUSS **...AND THE CIRCUS LEAVES TOWN** 1995

ELECTRIC WIZARD **ELECTRIC WIZARD** 1995

REVELATION **...YET SO FAR** 1995

SLO BURN **AMUSING THE AMAZING** 1996

FU MANCHU **IN SEARCH OF...** 1996

CATHEDRAL **HOPKINS (THE WITCHFINDER GENERAL)** 1997

ACRIMONY **TUMULI SHROOMAROOM** 1997

THE HEADS **EVERYBODY KNOWS WE GOT NOWHERE** 1997

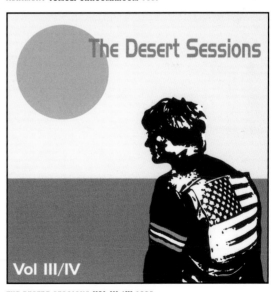

THE DESERT SESSIONS **VOL III/IV** 1998

IRON MONKEY **OUR PROBLEM** 1998

SLEEP **JERUSALEM** 1998

8

PLANET ROCK

At first glance, you could be forgiven for thinking that very little has changed in the world of metal since the early days — sex and violence are still the staple diet of the metal cover — but look a little closer and you will see that metal has come a long way.

The healthy dose of new influences injected into metal by the alternative scene must take the credit for spawning what became known as nu-metal, but it is the Adidas-obsessed band Korn that is recognized as the godfather of the scene. Korn have little respect for the old-guard classic metal acts. As far as they are concerned, their musical influences begin with the music of Faith No More and the Red Hot Chili Peppers. Black Sabbath, Iron Maiden, Saxon, Judas Priest, the Scorpions: these bands mean little to them, and if some metal fans consider such a claim blasphemous, they should remember that this is just the kind of anti-establishment attitude that is the foundation of all great heavy metal.

Visually, it is not possible to see exactly how Korn's anonymously titled debut album from 1994 can be aligned with past metal classics. Indeed, on paper, having a child on the cover playing on a swing gives the reader the impression that Korn are a pop group targeting the pre-teen market. However, the menace that pours out of this simple image keeps up the metal tradition of scaring the hell out of parents, and ensures that most pre-teens would be far too terrified of the band to even utter their name.

The album cover to Limp Bizkit's 1997 classic *Three Dollar Bill Y'All* marks a major turning point in metal's history. It signalled the end of an era, and the dawn of a whole

KORN KORN 1994

new look for metal fans. Just as when glam metal saw off the denim and leather of classic metal, nu-metal saw the end of the DM boot and combat trouser look that had risen to cult status with the birth of thrash metal. Within months of this album's release, metal kids adopted the new look of excessively baggy, immeasurably long jeans, expensive sneakers, baggy T-shirts, and, most notably, short hair. Previously, acts such as Anthrax, Aerosmith, Rage Against The Machine, and the Red Hot Chili Peppers had brought hip-hop to the attention of metal fans, but none of them had persuaded the kids that dressing like hip-hop fans was a viable option. And any metal fan that cut their hair prior to the birth of nu-metal was obviously betraying their roots, or worse, getting a job in a bank. With *Three Dollar Bill Y'All*, all that changed. Suddenly it was okay to cut your hair and wear it short. In fact, it was more than okay; it was necessary, in order to distance yourself from the old-guard metal bands, so long lambasted by every other genre as hoary old dinosaurs.

But Limp Bizkit weren't the only band to win the hearts and minds of metal fans. Marilyn Manson's brand of goth-meets-headbanger-meets-travelling-freak-show couldn't fail to capture the attention of metal fans with the cover of 1998's *Mechanical Animal*. And, if some people foolishly like to imagine Manson the most demonic character ever to have sprung from the depths of heavy metal's bowels, they would do well to remember the terror that metal legends Ozzy Osbourne, Alice Cooper, Glen Benton, et al struck into the hearts of local religious and youth groups whenever they passed through town. That said, *Mechanical Animal* is a design classic, a work of art in itself that would not look out of place hanging in modern art museums the world over. The same certainly couldn't be said of Ozzy Osbourne's *Bark At The Moon*.

Talking of freaks, let us not forget Mortiis, the one-time bass player in black metal legends Emperor who, as can clearly be seen on the cover of his 2001 album *The Smell Of Rain*, gladly suffers hours in make-up applying the face of a troll onto his own once corpse-painted scowl. Slipknot, on the other hand, make it easy on themselves by

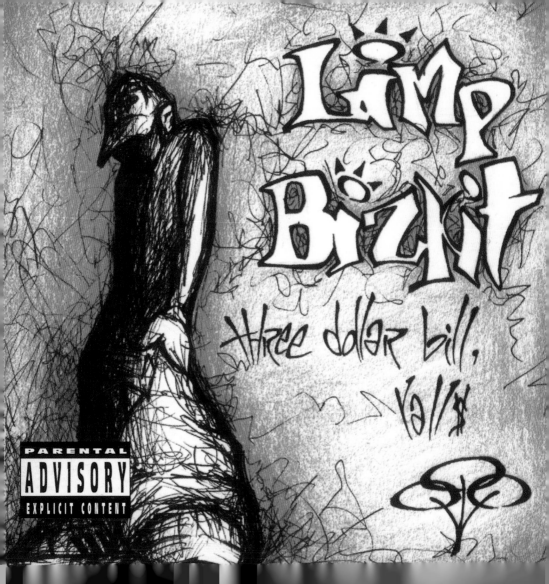

...oosing to appear as a unit dressed only in boiler suits, and their now instantly
...ognizable masks, as seen on their 1999 debut album *Slipknot*, proves that death metal
...ot dead just yet.

Plenty of today's metal acts are proud to be metal bands, and continue to use
...ssic metal elements in their album cover design. Take High On Fire's 2005 album,
...ssed Black Wings. There can be no mistaking this album for anything other than what it
...heavy metal. Amen's *We Have Come For Your Parents*, released in 2000, nods its head at
...ck Sabbath's classic religious parody cover *Heaven and Hell*, and Disturbed's *Believe*
...m 2002 reinvigorates the used and abused pentagram motif. Of course, Damageplan's
...w Found Power harks back to album covers from the thrash metal era; however, instead
...using the foreboding image of a mushroom cloud as a shock tactic, they use it as a
...taphor for the band's power. Damageplan's members stride forth like some kind of heavy
...tal Fantastic Four, born from the terrible raw energy of an atom bomb.

One cover that could easily slip under the radar is HIM's *Love Metal* from 2003.
...before you flick past it, consider that this image is a perfect example of the new life
...t is being breathed into metal today. This kind of satirical cover, a combination of a love
...rt and the satanic five-pointed pentagram, would have been unimaginable in the latter
...t of the 20th century – HIM would have been heavily criticized for insulting metal and
...bands that really took their satanic imagery to heart. Today, this merging of
...ntagram and love heart does more to describe metal fans' love for the music than
...ds ever could, and has exactly the right amount of self-deprecation to appeal to fans of
...tal, young and old.

And so, over 30 years since Black Sabbath first unleashed the beast, heavy
...tal is still thriving, still defying its critics, still raising hell, still offending those in
...itions of authority, and it looks like its here to stay. Long live heavy metal. Long live
...metal album cover!

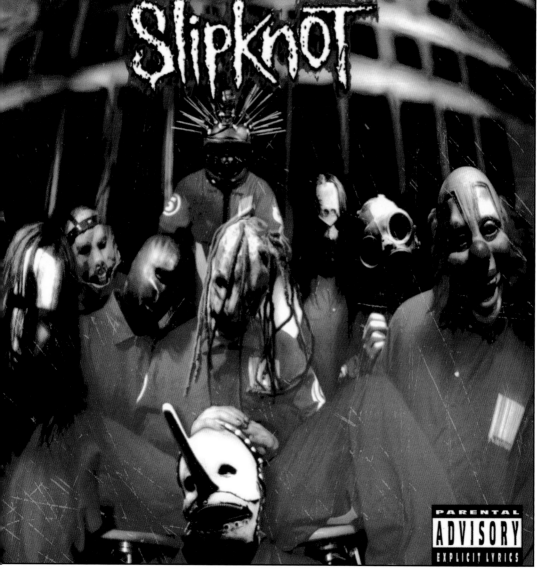

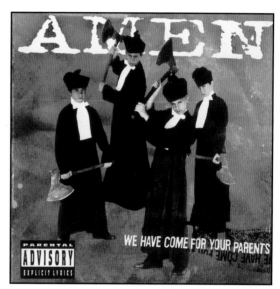

LINKIN PARK **HYBRID THEORY** 2000   AMEN **WE HAVE COME FOR YOUR PARENTS** 2000

NASHVILLE PUSSY **HIGH AS HELL** 2000
SYSTEM OF A DOWN **TOXICITY** 2001

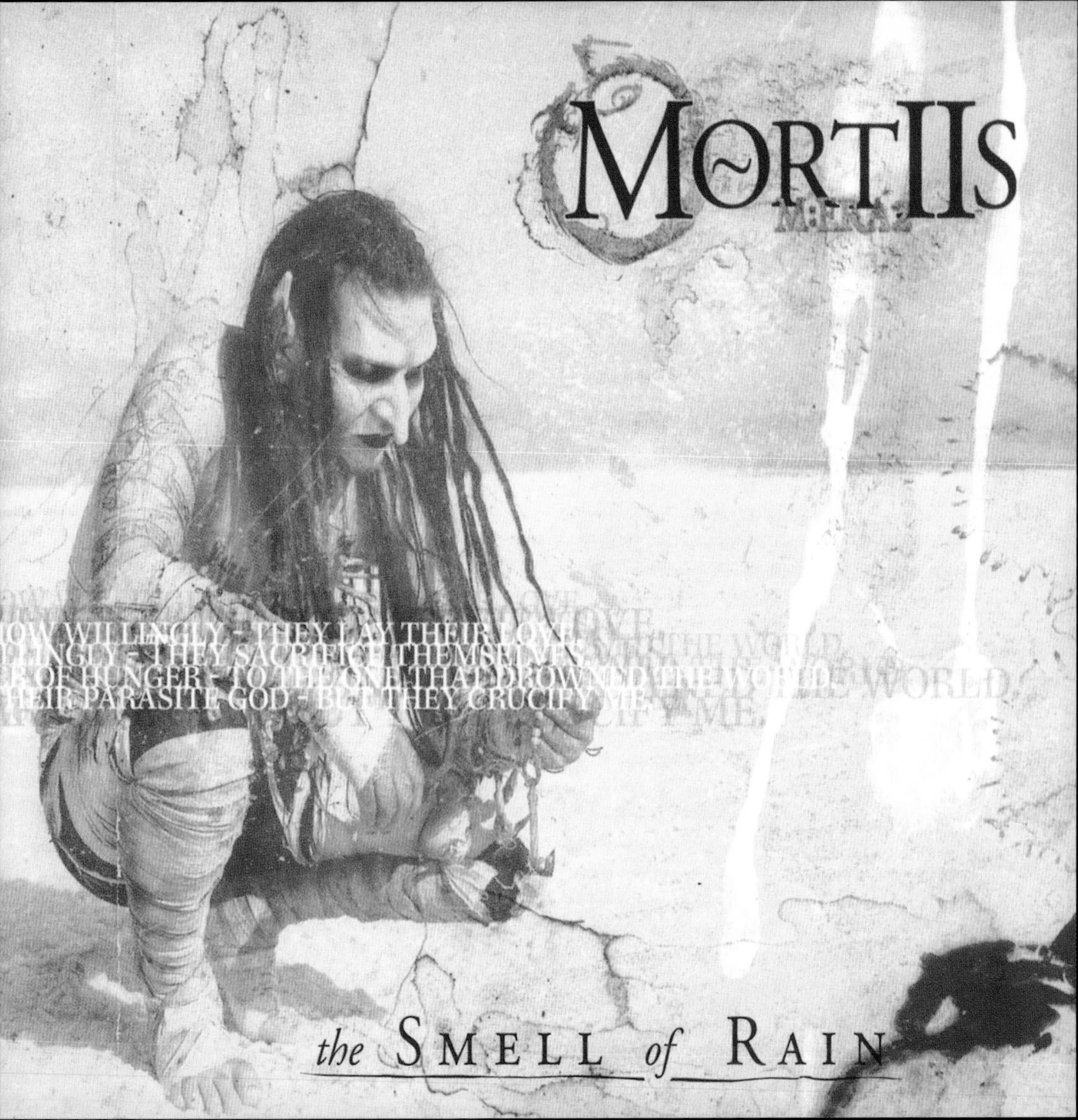

MORTIIS
OW WILLINGLY - THEY LAY THEIR LOVE
LLINGLY - THEY SACRIFICE THEMSELVES
R OF HUNGER - TO THE ONE THAT DROWNED THE WORLD
HEIR PARASITE GOD - BUT THEY CRUCIFY ME
the SMELL of RAIN

MORTIIS THE SMELL OF RAIN 2001

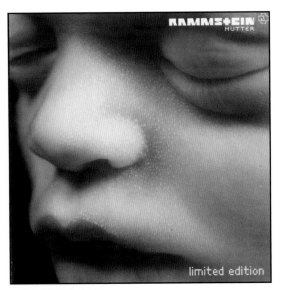

RAMMSTEIN **MUTTER** 2001

PAPA ROACH **LOVEHATETRAGEDY** 2002

DISTURBED **BELIEVE** 2002

HIM **LOVE METAL** 2003

DAMAGEPLAN **NEW FOUND POWER** 2004

LOSTPROPHETS **START SOMETHING** 2004

MASTODON **LEVIATHAN** 2004

PROBOT **PROBOT** 2004

ARCH ENEMY **DOOMSDAY MACHINE** 2004

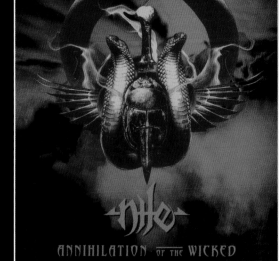

HIGH ON FIRE **BLESSED BLACK WINGS** 2005

NILE **ANNIHILATION OF THE WICKED** 2005

SLUNT
GET A LOAD OF THIS

BATTLE HYMNS 1982

AFTERWORD

Finally, it would be impossible to compile a book about heavy metal album covers and not have an in-depth look at Manowar. The band formed when bassist Joey DeMaio – who was then working as a bass and pyro technician for Black Sabbath – met guitarist Ross The Boss, whose then-band Shaking Street were supporting Sabbath on a UK tour. Manowar went straight for the metal jugular, producing a debut album, *Battle Hymns*, in 1982 that was among the best, majestic metal ever to be recorded. Manowar have built on a reputation of being more metal than any other band in the world, no mean feat when you consider the calibre of the competition. Though *Battle Hymns* brought them to the attention of record-buying metal maniacs around the world, it was the release of their follow-up album on Megaforce Records in 1983 that proved they meant business. Signing their record contract in blood (the first band recognized to do so), Manowar appeared on the front cover of *Into Glory Ride* wearing leather and loin cloths and brandishing swords. This, together with lyrics like "Hear the pounding army of the night, The call of metal summons us tonight, And gather we on this site, To behold the power and the might, We wear leather, we wear spikes, we rule the night" from the track "Gloves Of Metal", cemented their reputation as a pure, 100% metal band.

Their detractors may see Manowar as something of a joke, an overblown metal act that takes itself far too seriously, but the band's dedication to the cause of metal cannot be laughed at. Their album covers are always totally metal; not once have they strayed from the path, and though that may bring derisive sneers from critics, their fans are exactly that – fanatical – writing to the band and signing off in their own blood in homage to the band's own dedication to the metal cause.

Aside from *Into Glory Ride*, Manowar's 1984 *Hail To England* containing all the elements of the traditional metal cover: a musclebound, leatherclad warrior armed with a blood-drenched sword hacks his way through hoardes of enemies, while his semi-naked, large-breasted woman kneels at his feet. Sexist, stereotyped, and miles away from the reality of the vast majority (if not all) of metal's fan's lives, *Hail To England* demonstrates everything that metal means to its lovers; it's a world of escapism where everyone is master of their own destiny, where no man bows down to another, where "fuck you" is indeed the motto enscribed on each and every metal fan's coat of arms.

If this wasn't enough to raise Manowar to the top of the metal world, their next album, 1984's *Sign Of The Hammer*, propelled the band into the Guiness Book Of Records as the loudest band in the world (recorded playing at 130 decibels), which more than makes up for having an album cover that is probably the least metal of all their output.

Hereafter, Manowar never failed to produce album covers that were the epitome of metal artwork. *Fighting The World*, from 1987, pictures the band as musclebound lords, wrapped in leather, fists raised high in salute as lightning flashes around them.

INTO GLORY RIDE 1983

HAIL TO ENGLAND 1984

SIGN OF THE HAMMER 1984

FIGHTING THE WORLD 1987

KINGS OF METAL 1988

THE TRIUMPH OF STEEL 1992

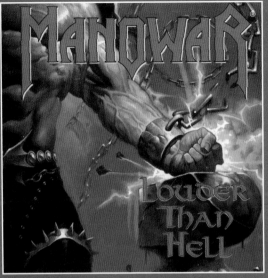

LOUDER THAN HELL 1996

WARRIORS OF THE WORLD 2002

Kings Of Metal (1988) is yet another classic metal album cover. Kings of Metal is also the title bestowed upon the band by their fans, which is surely justified by their album cover artwork alone, since no other heavy metal band can claim *never* to have swayed from the metal path, either musically or visually.

The Triumph Of Steel (1992) however, must be the greatest of all their covers. Just how metal can you get? The lyrics to "Metal Warriors (Brothers Of Metal Part II)" say it all:

> There's magic in metal,
> There's magic in us all,
> Heavy metal or no metal at all,
> Wimps and posers leave the hall,
> Death to false metal!